Unveiling Self

a collection of student memoirs

Leslie St. John

Table of Contents

Introduction

"There are few human beings who receive the truth, complete and staggering, by instant illumination. Most of them acquire it fragment by fragment, on a small scale, by successive developments, cellularly, like a laborious mosaic."

~Anaïs Nin

As a writing teacher of twelve years, I have always emphasized expressive arguments through personal narratives. Over the years, thousands of essays about Grandma's cooking, hunting trips, surfing, and soccer injuries have come across my desk. But in 2012, I noticed a change. These new essays were well-written, yes, but also honest—bone-dense. At the center of each essay was an insistence on grappling with personal truth. What I was reading was real. I wanted to acknowledge the merit of these essays with more than just a fine grade. I wanted to amplify the voices of these burgeoning writers, and let others hear.

How to do this within the confines of a University Educational System? Step outside. Prioritize relationships first, and see what might emerge with collaboration among a teacher and student writers. *Unveiling Self* is the result of many conversations we held while sitting around my kitchen table or on the living room floor, meeting in cafes, and messaging on a Facebook group page. This book truly is a co-creation between myself and eighteen students from different backgrounds and majors.

The project is three years in the making, full of starts and halts. As memoir is based in truth, some students withdrew their essays. While students may write bravely for a teacher, it is an entirely other experience to know family, coaches, and peers may read this honest account. As the years progressed, we all lived with the uncertainty. Would we complete the project? But something kept us going. The final essays were hard earned. The students made many revisions, incorporating feedback from each other. Giving these essays a home in a self-designed, published book to read and share with others is an exciting accomplishment. While I can't speak for the students, I can say that *something* for me was simple: I wanted to honor their words.

Within the pages of *Unveiling Self*, you will read about family—dynamics, divorce, how we define ourselves in relation to or in opposition from our parents; the body—masculine/feminine cultural expectations, scars, illness; and the Self: that capital "S" sense of inner knowing. These essays ask tough questions about perfectionism, drugs, approval, brokenness, and personal power. Some are humorous, such as José Parra's "Dancing with Myself," in which he says, "The vast majority of stupid or spontaneous things that I have done in my life can be explained in five words: It was for a girl." Some are meditative, as in Katherine Seth's "The Gold Family," where she uses *Kintsugi*, the ancient Japanese art of repairing broken pottery with gold, as a metaphor to understand the beauty in her own brokenness: "I know now that my brokenness is not something of which to be ashamed, nor is it my defining characteristic. It is a single aspect of myself, an aspect to be celebrated because it is one of the many pieces that makes me who I am."

Beyond rich content, these writers experimented with structural narrative. Erica Barrios' essay, "All Things in Contact with the Sea" uses italicized sections to fold the narrator's oceanic, lyrical interior into the story. She writes, "I paddle farther out, hasty to arrive at the break. I spend its duration submerged, water thickening the pages of books I've collected in my head, their black text slipping off—letter by letter into the sea." Many essays use extended metaphors to frame their subjects: dreaming reality, riding a bike, getting off the lunge line, watching a film, and so on. In these essays, you will recognize fiction techniques, such as scene and summary, dialogue, characterization, as well as nonfiction hallmarks: image, memory, observation, and reflection. All of the essays leave me with a tangible impression of what it is to be in process with the Self.

The truths these writers discovered may have come in fragments, pieces of memory blurring into images, voices, and histories; but what they have offered here is a cohesive collection of how they see the world and are unveiling their place within it. In what feels like a bedrock essay in the collection, Jillian Elisberg's piece "The Final Stage of Healing," reveals her acute subjectivity in relation to the college campus collective:

> Hundreds of people passed me every day and saw my scar. I was not a green-eyed, blond-haired, petite female. I was a walking scar. My mind felt irrelevant; my scar was the first thing people talked to me about. I could tell you about every single episode of *Good Eats*, the way swimming long distances makes me feel expansive, or Stephen Hawking's description of gravity using ball bearings. Unfortunately, on a college campus filled with thousands of strangers, what you see is what you get. I was my all-consuming scar.

I am humbled to read such raw reflection, such authorial confidence. These essays...*all* of them are brave journeys into the Self. We invite you to remove the veil and read. Story by story and fragment by fragment, may you see what we saw, and in that looking, recognize parts of yourself.

Leslie St. John
4/17/2015

Memoirs

All Things in Contact with the Sea

By: Erica Margueritte Barrios

> **"My body rests on the surface, testing the balance of my current surrender and my former struggle."**

I do not know if the ocean began in calm or chaos. If the calm began and manifested into a stubborn uproar, or the chaos settled into a seldom moving still, the only assurance is these junctures blend into each other with devotion. Either way, all things in contact with the sea choose to yield with or struggle against it.

This thought consumes me as I shoot my eyes in the direction of the glassy water and let my body follow. Shock shrouds the tips of my toes as the cold works its way up to fan out my hair in suspended tendrils. The sea swallows me whole until my surfboard's leash yanks my ankle, a reminder to come up for the last moments of the break. The sea moves toward me in a sequence of waves that form and fall apart with a crash over my washed out arms and legs. I cannot fight the change in my state of being as it mimics the temperament of the water. One wave, two waves, three, four. When will the water still? I count five more.

Collectively the nine of us Barrios kids experienced a childhood destined to be recreated on film, as my mother juggled the upbringings of nine children on her own. From an outside standpoint this doesn't seem unbearable— this non-traditional family dynamic is reminiscent of a Wes Anderson movie until you're a member of one. Imagine.

One, mom. Dad gone. Room, clean, not my mess. Glass, broken, not my fault. Allan, glass, artery, ambulance. Friends, not inside, messy house, empty fridge. Christmas, fifty-four gifts. Fallen tree, *Craig? Where'd you go?* Laughter. Dinner table, carne asada, four at a time. Finish, go, next. Punishment, backyard, all locked out, 90 degrees. Mom, exhausted, room, prohibited. Brandon, hide and seek, dryer, banned. Lego, chin, me, stiches. Soccer, Rick, cast, 3 months, pale leg. Eric, dances, sings, no injuries. Gymnastics, dance, acting. Nine pairs of track shoes. Nine of everything.

Persistent waves. Although I know the duration of the waves rivals the break, I endure as if it is twice as long. I hug my board in surrender, falling into a tilting motion. Left, right, left, right.

Our bodies swayed towards each side of the car. Turns pushed us in the direction of the passenger side only to reverse towards my Mother in her fist-shaking, wide-eyed state. Spanish words escaping her mouth with each impatient light turning red before she could speed through. Words I won't repeat. Our range of motion ending only by the body placed in the next seat or less comfortably, by the window. "Maybe if we left earlier I wouldn't need to drive like a maniac." An argument arising between my mom and one of my brothers. "You can't even leave the house before 8:10 yourself Mom!" Momentarily all voices would chime in as a potpourri of complaints seeping through my attempt to filter out noise from quiet. As the right-most illuminated number on the dashboard changed with each passing minute the swaying progressed to jerking, bickering to howling. I forced the intake of air deep into my lungs and held it in acquiescence for the remainder of the drive.

"Hurry up, you'll be late!" My mother's voice shot at my ears, a starter gun upon arrival. I hotfooted it across the street separating my house and the schoolyard. Flying into an office only to be greeted with reproach by Mrs. Such and Such, who filled each passing day with tardy slips and the sharpening of pencils. I followed her hand to the "unexcused" box on a tiny yellow piece of paper as a miniscule but menacing checkmark materialized. "How do you manage to be late every day making your way from 9337 to 9338 Gotham Street?" I remained silent while her incessant orangey-red lips separated and closed. "It's just across the street, for heaven's sake." I snatched the paper, walked to class ransacking my mind for a way to navigate the chaos that manifested at home.

Hands meet the sea to propel me out of reach of the swaying van, my red-faced frustration: rugged waters. I paddle farther out, hasty to arrive at the break. I spend its duration submerged, water thickening the pages of books I've collected in my head, their black text slipping off- letter by letter into the sea. I surface in an attempt to recollect. The words of my father swim back and pour in through my ears as ink.

"Here's a novel about Lewis and Clark. There's a lot to be learned from history," said the man who could not make sense of his own volatile past with my mother. I nodded at my father on the first time I'd seen him in years. "Harry Potter isn't the real world, Erica, how come you can recite lines from books filled with nonsense, but not any facts." "Because I don't like facts, and I don't care what you think," I responded. Later I tucked Lewis and Clark on the bookshelf, only touching it again to place it in the "One dollar" pile of books at my Mom's garage sale. I was saving money for my next escape— the newest Harry Potter novel or something similar to add to my collection. The fantastical worlds in these books took me in, as I snuck out from underneath the pile of my grappling siblings with my mother perched at the top holding a grass stained flag made of soccer uniforms and dirty socks. This eagerness to escape imbedded itself into my actions as I placed myself in books of my choosing and lived in them like temporary homes.

Waves turn over in navy blue as yellowing pages begin a descent towards a fatal crash. Saturated by salt the pages scatter and sink to the bottom. Taken in by the uproarious sea myself I watch while the waves tumble me on their highest setting. I can make no attempt to rescue my drowning worlds.

"Get out of this house, I'm sick of your shit," my mother's voice shot up towards the ceiling. My offense could range from anything between a dirty cup on the counter to having my headphones in. I looked at the areas surrounding her body without a word; my awkward eye contact with the floor and walls intensified her volume as I avoided her gaze. These lectures were time invested into my pursuit for tranquillity. My mother listed my grievances against her while I mapped out my escape from the overfilled house, the arguments.

William gave my mom the finger at sixteen; Craig quietly sulked away at seventeen, the rest of my siblings around eighteen. At seventeen my turn was coming. My mother had set her sights on me: first came name-calling, among the impromptu arguments, then threats to be kicked out. Like each of my brothers I reached a point where the decision to leave was of my own accord. When my situation breached the out of control, I put my few possessions into the car—and finally

left home. I fled with the belief that withdrawing from those

surroundings would disentangle me from the turmoil I experienced all

my life.

I continue to paddle out but the break evades me. With the distance

I achieve comes the consciousness that turmoil lives inside me. My

books sank, the waves will not cease. Where would I be if I stopped

running away...back in this upheaval? Am I allowing myself to escape

momentarily because this is simpler than finding the true solution? Am

I still doing this now? I paddle faster away until my arms shake: I give

in to the waves that continually crash and see I no longer consider

escape a friend.

Deep breath, Chaturanga, and my arms are still shaking. I occupy

six by four feet of the polished wooden ground in a yoga studio. Sitting,

standing, lunging, flowing, allowing revival to sneak in with oxygen

while I breathe. My body forces thoughts out with the arrival of

physical strain, focus on consistent breathing, still body- balanced

mind. The end of the class brings ultimate stillness as we lie on our

backs in Savasana, gravity willing our bodies flat into the floor. The

yoga instructor's flowing voice speaks of all things vital, but today words weave in and out of my consciousness in disarray. "Let the stillness overtake you, revert to your natural state."

Natural state. Am I calm or chaotic by nature?

I know we're supposed to cleanse our minds, give thoughts leave and allow their departure. I know all this, but my memories are rocks tossed carelessly to create whatever ripples they may in my clarity. Hours pass in introspection, as I sort out my place amidst the images of car rides, messy shared bedrooms, and dark places filled with thought. Reading, moving out, the ocean: all ineffective forms of escape. I lie on the floor with these thoughts, a little late but finally arriving at a long awaited rendezvous with the past. I come to terms with my personal chaos by being fully present in it.

Now basking in the break, the waves have given me the strength to be still. My body rests on the surface, testing the balance of my current surrender and my former struggle. I do not know the order in which the calm or chaos began. I do not know if I was born into serenity, or chaos filled my soul from its creation. My acquaintance with turmoil forced me to find silence in my tumultuous life. Surviving my chaos means bringing the calm along when the waves hit.

The Ride

By: Tara Baumann

> *"I felt like that was all I could do—deal with an issue that I didn't understand by just being quiet and waiting for it to end."*

I never learned how to ride a bike. My dad bought my sister and me each a bike when we moved to California but he never taught me how to ride mine. He taught my sister how to ride hers when we were still living in New York, but I was too young back then. Then when we moved to California, he didn't have the time. My mom's excuse for not teaching me was that she wasn't "strong enough" to catch me if I fell. That excuse has followed me like a shadow ever since. I've always felt like no one is strong enough to catch me if I fall.

I was ten years old when my dad left. My sister and I didn't talk to him for two years after that. During those two years, my mom wasn't strong enough for anything. She sat in bed and ate white cheddar popcorn from Trader Joe's and Vitamin Water for a whole summer. She lost sixty pounds and the majority of her connection to the world outside of her head. She didn't understand why my dad left. None of us did. He told her it was because he felt like he had only stayed in the marriage as long as he did "out of obligation, not love." That almost killed her. As summer came to a close so did my mom's time in the dark about why her husband left.

My sister hacked into a secret email account of my father's that she and my mom had discovered when trying to book a flight with his account for us to visit our family on the east coast. In this account she found a whole other life of our father's. A secret world my father had been living in for years that none of us knew anything about. She showed these emails to my mom and they locked themselves in our upstairs office, glued to the computer screen, in a glazed state of mourning. They were constantly either up in there reading, or in my mom's tissue-littered bedroom together talking and crying. My sister was fourteen years old and had to act like a therapist for my forty-some-odd year old manic-depressive mother. I was eleven with no honest idea as to what was happening to my family and how I was supposed to be affected by it. All I knew was that my dad was the enemy and that my mom and sister had some painful secret that I was "too young" to know about because it had to do with sex and "YOUR FATHER'S FUCKING WHORES." I felt alone. I felt naïve. I felt powerless. I was falling and I knew that no one could catch me.

I never read the emails. I came across a thick folder one day in the garage that was filled with printed emails and ads; I knew what it was—

it was every piece of text that I knew would strike my eyes like glass on concrete and shatter into a million cracked pieces of what I knew would be hatred and disgust for the man that raised me. I couldn't bring myself to sit down and read it all. I knew that I had the power to finally know the details of what it was that my mom and sister were always whispering about behind closed doors—but I just couldn't do it. The thought of my dad being this twisted sex-crazed sociopathic other being was too beyond comprehension for me. I wouldn't let myself see him as someone else, so I made myself see him as nobody; I erased him to the point of ancient and incomprehensible history. He was a painful nothing to me that I would not talk about and I would not remember, until I finally had to.

I was in seventh grade when I stopped going to school. I had erased my dad. I stopped eating. I stopped being the nice person that I always had been. I just flat out stopped caring. My world consisted of lying in bed, eating the occasional rice cake, sitting in hours of therapy every week acting like I was unaffected by it all, and constantly being sick (probably due to the lack of nutritional value in my diet mixed with the depression). I don't remember what I thought about most days. I had gone to this fancy private school since kindergarten, but I ended up being "asked to leave" in the middle of my seventh grade year because of my excessive absences.

I was at the airport with my mom and sister when we got the call from my principal essentially telling me that I had to find a new school and friends. I had already been feeling like I didn't belong when I was at home, then hearing that I had to be that weird kid that comes into a new school in the middle of the year for "personal reasons" was just going to make everything worse. My mom and sister were yelling at me about my attendance and how I had "done this to [myself]" when we were standing in the middle of the airport waiting to get onto a flight back to Los Angeles from visiting my mom's parents. My mom bought two seats together on the plane and one seat seven rows back. She said, "I had planned on having you and your sister sit together but I don't think either of us want to sit next to you for six hours after this shit. You can be by yourself and think about your fucking bullshit and what you've done for a while. Don't talk to me. Don't even look at me." I pinched myself to stop any emotions from leaking onto my face and with the most sincere-looking and douche-baggy bravery said, "Sounds fucking perfect." I didn't want to sit alone. We walked onto the plane, exchanged a few glares, and took our seats. My seat fell near the back of the plane and my mom and sister's were more toward the center. I had the middle seat in my row. I was between an older man and a sleeping middle-aged woman.

That man ended up molesting me, and I was too afraid to say a word. I was just about thirteen years old and I had never been touched by a boy my own age before and I had definitely never been touched by a grown man. He finally stopped and fell asleep. I was in this mental frenzy of not knowing what to do or say or feel—I awoke the woman sitting on the other side of me and gave her a letter telling her that the man to my right had been touching me. I didn't know what to do since my family was rows ahead, and I didn't want to involve them. She demanded that we switch seats and when we landed she found my mom and told her what happened, against my will…I wanted to keep it to myself. I don't know if it was out of shame for having sat there in silence or because I didn't want my mom to know that I still needed someone to care about me and take care of me—someone to hold onto me and make me feel safe when I start to fall. My mom didn't even believe her at first. She thought I was looking for attention—that really fucking hurt. As we got off of the plane and walked down Terminal 6, with my mom finally believing what happened and processing the fact that she should find a police officer, my sister was there giving me shit for not having said something to the man—she said it was my own fault and that I should have just screamed and gotten him in trouble with the air marshal. Yeah. In retrospect I probably should have done that. But for some reason the whole time it was going on I was experiencing the same striking feeling of helplessness and being too weak or young or small to stand up and say something for myself that I had been feeling ever since my dad left. I felt voiceless. I had gotten so used to being pushed aside, falling down, and being left to deal with issues I didn't really understand at such a young age, that I felt like that was all I could do—deal with an issue that I didn't understand by just being quiet and waiting for it to end.

I moved in with my dad for seven months shortly after I had fallen from my hellish flight down to a turbulent LAX. I didn't talk to my mom or sister the entire time I was living with him. After two years of no contact, I moved in with my father and his pregnant girlfriend/fiancé, Nikita, (he never was too clear on their relationship status) and her son from her current husband because I felt too out of place with my mother and sister and too resentful of them. Nikita was nice to me. She seemed like she actually wanted to spend time with me. I thought she was like a sort of motherly friend to me despite how much my actual mother hated her very existence. But it seemed like she made my dad happy in a way that I hadn't really seen before; it wasn't a better sort of happiness, it was different.

I was only thirteen years old when Nikita asked me, "Have you ever smoked weed before sweetie?" "Uh yeah a bunch of times with some friends." That was a lie. I think I lied because the side of me that saw her as a friend wanted her approval and thought that she would think I was cool or something if I had friends that smoked weed. The only mind-altering substance I had consumed before that time was whatever bit of frozen strawberry margarita my dad would share with me each time I caught him making them. I didn't have friends to do anything with, let alone smoke weed, after switching schools. Even before the school-switch, my friends were not the type to get high—I was a national spelling bee champ by fifth grade with acceptances to schools for "gifted children" from all over Los Angeles, and my old friends were definitely cut from the same overachieving-cloth. Nikita left the room to get some weed but came back with more than just that. "So I was rummaging through your dad's armoire and found three tabs of ecstasy leftover from Hailey Duff's birthday party a few months ago. Wanna split them?" I didn't even know what in the hell ecstasy was. Well, we did it and I found out later that she was a stripper and "ex"-prostitute that was only with my dad for his money and used me as a way to get closer to him. I had some issues dealing with that....all of that. I moved back in with my mom and sister not too long after our night of drugs and alcohol.

I wish I could say that through all of this I learned that the love of a family, no matter how broken it may grow to be, is always strong enough to build back up and allow the members to make peace and love each other again. But I will never love any of them the same way I did before April of 2005, when my dad's move out of the family began. I can't even say the words "I love you" to my parents even though years have passed, and they believe me to be "over it." I don't think I will ever be honestly over it. I know "we're all human." We all make mistakes that hurt people. And I can forgive all of the wrongs of my parents, but I cannot let all of them go. I am not sure I can have a relationship with either of them because I just don't feel connected to them anymore. We have a general understanding of each other, and where each of us stands with the other, so we make our relationships work as what they are.

I have learned that no good comes from staying quiet or letting yourself and your feelings be unheard. After living through and learning from the experiences in which I have been weak, I wish I could say that I have finally and fully learned how to be strong and catch myself when I am falling. But the truth is that I'm still learning, I'm in this free-fall and I don't think I'll ever be done gaining something out of each part of the lesson I plunge into. I can't be ready to pick myself up from the unexpected disasters the universe may have in store for me but with each tough time I will get more and more able to pick myself up, take in some fresh air, and get right back onto riding down the turn-coated path of life in a healthy way.

Finding the Pride

By: Tal Edelstein

> *"The air-raid siren blares. All the emergency-protocols practiced at school suddenly fled my mind like panicked birds."*

Fifteen seconds. That's all the time I had to drop what I was doing and find the nearest shelter. With the air-raid siren wailing in my ear, I sprinted for my life. Women screaming, children crying. Fragmented sounds shrieking like the fragmented sentences I am composing. The air-raid siren blares. All the emergency-protocols practiced at school suddenly fled my mind like panicked birds. Chaos was everywhere as I sat in the bomb shelter. Looking across the valley on my way home, I saw a scene out of a horror movie. Enormous black plumes of smoke billowed from the Haifa train station, planes and helicopters with the Star of David tattooed to their side racing to the counterstrike; the Second Lebanon War had escalated. "AZAKA!" [1] my dad yelled so often that it has become engraved in my muscles to anxiously jerk my head anytime I hear it. Hundreds of hours over the following thirty-four days were spent waiting in a shelter. I couldn't even finish a video game or family dinner because of the constant need to run for cover. Thousands of rockets were fired into my country, some falling on my own street. By the age of ten, I had seen what many don't see their entire lives. At the age of ten, I had my first encounter with pure hatred, the first of many steps towards a complete transformation of myself from a shy, embarrassed child to a prideful, confident Israeli adult.

Living through a war while having kids must have traumatized my parents, because only a year and a half later we left Israel for America, leaving everything behind, including the branched-out family I had grown up with my whole life. It was especially hard for my grandparents to see us go, and before we left, my Savta [2] gave me a Star of David necklace. My only memory of that moment was how shiny and pretty the hexagram was, with its six sharp points gleaming from the overhead chandelier light – but it really had no meaning to me. It was just a symbol of my country, my religion, my people – something that was so naturally occurring to me while living in Israel, that it had no vivid influence on me. I tucked it into my shirt when I got dressed the next morning, and thought nothing of it.

I struggled with the transition to the US. It was a completely different environment: different people, different words, different food, different thoughts and attitudes, different values, different religion, different culture. Where I was used to seeing people yelling at each other to hurry up the line at the supermarket, I now saw kind people who would wait three hours for the old lady to cross the road. Instead of Hebrew I heard English. Instead of the local corner falafel kiosk, I saw an In-N-Out store on every street. Everything in America was so by the book and following the rules – a mindset completely different from Israel's "go with the flow" attitude, where the daily hectic chaos became a calming norm. The one thing that wasn't different was basketball.

I had played basketball growing up in Israel, and it was one of the few things I had in common with my new 6th grade classmates. "Hey, Jew! Come play and maybe we'll toss you a quarter." I caught the ball by the three point line, and the kid defending me reached out as if to slap the ball, but instead grabbed my necklace and ripped it off me. I quickly picked it up off the ground and slipped it in my pocket without saying a word or making eye contact with him. I felt his hands strategically place themselves on my back, and as I tumbled down to the ground my eyes, welling up with tears. I was surrounded by a pack of vultures who had just spotted their dinner. The bell rang. I was left alone on the blacktop.

My parents were worried about mine and my sister's difficulty in acclimating to our new home. My dad, having grown up in America, decided that the best solution would be to send us to Camp Ramah in

California, a Jewish summer camp. My sister and I were very against the idea, claiming that we were just being sent to another American prison, but this time only on a smaller scale than the country itself. Begrudgingly, we were sent off. Begrudgingly, we acted our way through the first day as if we were actually enjoying ourselves. But when I saw my sister later that night, we both just cried together and talked about escaping and moving back to Israel – a thought that seemed plausible in the minds of a thirteen and eleven year olds.

We came back. I was a camper there for three more years, and this summer will be my third year as a staff member there. During that first summer, I finally found a community that I identified with. Within the rolling hills of the Ventura mountains, hidden in the tiny town of Ojai, California, was the place that I would soon come to call my second home. 600 people who I shared words, food, thoughts and attitudes, values, religion, and culture with, who are all drawn back summer after summer. For the past six years, anytime someone asked me what I was doing this summer, without an ounce of hesitation I would answer, "I'm going to camp." The most important thing that camp does for me is that it makes me feel comfortable with my religion and my culture in a land where less than 1% of people share that feeling with me. I was able to turn myself from a shy immigrant to a naturally loud and obnoxious

Israeli who happens to live in America. I learned how to be myself. But more important than that, I learned to be intensely proud of who I am.

The summer sun bounced its rays off my face as we drove back home along the 126. I was wiping the tears from my face when my mom looked back at me in her rearview mirror. "Tal, we need to get your necklace cleaned. It looks like it got really dirty over the summer." I looked down and saw that the shiny, silver Star of David had faded, and had a brown tint from a combination of four weeks of sweat and dirt. But it still had the shimmering sun to light it up as it nestled itself on the crumpled waves of my shirt. Only a few months prior, my necklace would be tucked into this cotton cave, hiding from the light.

My dad slammed the fridge door shut and walked over to his unofficially claimed chair. "Tal, you can't go. You need to focus on applying to colleges and making sure your grades stay high so that you can get in. And what about your basketball? You're just going to give up on that? Besides, we don't even have the money for it." I had heard about a trip called March of the Living during my first summer as a counselor, and I decided then and there that it was something I had to do. Over the previous years, my passion and pride for Israel and Judaism had only increased, and when I heard about this two week trip to Poland and Israel in memory of the Holocaust and in celebration of

Israeli Independence Day, I knew that it was something that I had to do. But as we sat in our homes conference room, the flames from the fireplace only made my dad's angry expression even scarier. He flashed back to his days as a lawyer, exuberantly fighting every point with a counterpoint. But I was too stubborn. I gave up basketball, got a job, and managed to scrap together the $6,300 I needed.

On April 23, 2014, I left for an experience that would change my life in the most powerful of ways. We toured the Warsaw Ghetto and the Warsaw Jewish Cemetery. We walked through the grounds of the Treblinka Death Camp. We prayed at a mass grave where 800 young Jewish children were brutally murdered in front of their parents – I got dehydrated from crying so much on that day. We went into Auschwitz-Birkenau, the most infamous of death camps from World War II, where we walked through rooms packed with shoes, suitcases, glasses, toys; where we walked through torture chambers and gas chambers with fingernails etched into the cement ceilings.

On the day of the International Holocaust Memorial Day, all of the March of the Living delegations gathered in Auschwitz to march the kilometers separating it from Birkenau. It had rained the night before, so the ground was incredibly muddy and slippery, but no one cared. We walked into the camp holding hands with the accompanying survivors, engulfed in Jewish youth and elder, proudly waving flags and singing in the same place where my people were nearly exterminated only a few decades earlier. "TAL EDELSTEIN! WHERE IS HE? WHERE IS TAL EDELSTEIN?" the leader of my delegation shouted. I knew Maya Cohen from camp, where she worked as a staff member when I was a camper. She knew how incredibly hard I had worked in order to be able to afford this trip. She stood with her arm around me as I cried at the mass grave for the children. She stayed back with me the day earlier at the far end of Birkenau, while the rest of our delegation headed back to the buses, so that I could have a few moments all to my own in probably the most religious experiences I have ever had in my life. She knew more than anyone how much March of the Living meant to me.

"Maya! Maya! I'm right here," I said, fearing that I was in trouble or that something bad had happened. "Tal, the Los Angeles delegation was, for the first time ever, selected to walk in front of the entire march, and I want you to be one of the fourteen representatives from LA to stand in front," she said. I was so honored that I just grabbed and squeezed her. But I was completely overwhelmed when she randomly selected the remaining thirteen representatives. She had singled me out and made me feel a pride that I had never felt before. I slowly walked by all the other delegations until I finally reached the front, standing underneath the camp entrance gate, where I was handed a flag and told to look serious for the cameras. I turned back, and saw the 11,000 people from 42 different countries that I was about to lead out of Auschwitz. I looked forward and saw the hundreds of reporters who had come to cover the event. I looked up at the flag that was in my hand, and saw the bright blue Star of David flapping in the wind, unafraid of showing who it was and what it stood for. The two triangles of the symbol interlocked in strength, despite all the pain and suffering it had been through. The six points standing sharp to protect its people from harm. The hexagon in the center symbolizing all of its people, unified as one, just like in Israel, just like in that elementary school playground, just like in Camp Ramah, and just like in this death camp in which I stood. Unified and proud.

A week later, all 11,000 of us were in Jerusalem, the capital city of Israel, celebrating the 66th Israeli Independence Day. As we all danced and sang on the march towards the Western Wall, my Star of David necklace bounced up and down on my shirt. I am that I am, and I am proud of what I am.

[1] Air raid siren
[2] Jewish grandmother

Hold It In

By: Maggie Thompson

> *"We share our vulnerability and our strengths through puffs of unconsolidated snapshots of a smoky past."*

We were sitting at a place called The Vortex. My heart was beating fast. The moon lit the night and my hands began to shake. Maybe it was nerves; maybe it was because it was 9°F outside and I had forgotten my mittens at home. Two older girls that I had met a few months earlier were sitting to my side talking about big things: the state of the union, the environmental problems facing our generation, other galaxies, and the end of the universe. The only thing on my mind was the weed in the girl's pocket next to me. We sat on the cement that overstretched the muddy Tittabawasee River. The Vortex was an old bridge. At one point it connected to the road on the other side of the river.

Morgan grabbed a Michigan-grown Honeycrisp apple from her purse, cut a crater into the top and began to make a pipe. Callie poked holes in the aluminium foil. I watched, wide eyed and nervous, feeling younger by the second. They kept talking. I kept listening. Morgan forcefully broke a pen open that we had stolen from our music teacher and slid it into the apple. She pulled out the bag of marijuana and smelled it. I took a whiff as she offered the bag to the end of my nose.

"Awful," I thought, "I'm about to smoke that?" She packed the hole

tight with the dried plant and gracefully handed the apple to me. "Go

ahead," she said while passing me a BIC lighter, "take the green." I

held the end of the pen to my lips and tried to light the weed. I fiddled

with the instrument, trying to get it to spark, feeling younger and

younger still. I should have been in diapers at this point. Morgan

smiled and took the lighter from me; upon sparking it she brought the

apple up to me and told me to breathe in. I did, filling my lungs with

reality, growth, and discovery of a new culture. "Hold it in," Callie said.

I did. I waited and let the smoke linger and make friends with my body.

They shared secrets of the past, and when I finally let my breathe out, I

let childhood and false wishes go. So there we were, legs hanging over

the edge of the frozen water, talking about things bigger than ourselves,

and I was happy.

Breathe it in.

I was fifteen at the time. Still learning about what it was like to

grow up, still deciding what kind of person I wanted to be. I spent so

many hours of my life on homework, at school, writing, reading,

adding, subtracting, and researching. My nights seemed too short for

how long my days were. It seemed as though I needed something to relax my overworked mind. The weed helped soothe the tension. It allowed for the night's short moments to linger, and allowed my relaxing evening to feel twice as long, twice as therapeutic. The slow, easy-listening music that played from the car radio those evenings seemed to resonate within me, mellow chord progressions vibrating through my veins and creating a warm head rush. In those moments, I wasn't worried about the grade I got on my geoscience test or when my English essay was due. I was disconnected from school and connected to those around me. I lived in the moment, not in the future, and certainly not in the past.

Hold it in.

My friends from previous years battled with their issues in other ways. Erin found her freedom in church, spending her free time helping out with the middle school program "Jesus and Me." In this program she learned, "don't have sex, don't do drugs, and don't have friends who think differently." Mary turned into a turtle as she stopped hanging out with us completely, spending all her time within the shell she created out of math books, chemistry labs, and Ernest Hemingway essays. Samantha's long, lean legs turned into pieces of floss as she controlled other parts of her life, such as food, to deal with the inconsistency of her stress. It seemed as though I was not doing anything different from them. We all deal with stress in different ways, but for some reason they didn't appreciate my choice of relief. Their faces turned from warm familiarity into whispers behind my back. Their presence no longer enjoyable, but instead a reminder of agonizing and jarring words from the kids in the hallways. "She smokes every day. I heard she got kicked out of Business Professionals of America. No, she isn't a Christian." The words still sound shrill in my ears.

I was sitting in the kitchen one day when Erin decided to stop by on her way home from the grocery store. We sat on the old dark wooden seats, drinking tea and talking about small thing: what kind of cupcakes she was going to make, New Year's resolutions, who she was taking to the Sadie Hawkin's dance. Just before she left, after we had taken our last sip of lukewarm tea she looked at me and asked, "How is deliberately getting new friends going?" I looked at her, into the abyss of her red-brown eyes. I thought back to the moments with Callie and Morgan and all my new friends. I thought about how my new friends would never think any differently of me, no matter what my life choices may be. Sure, Nick Murphy will drink a little too much whisky, and sometimes Ashley will kiss a few boys, then a few more— but no one was doing anything wrong. We were all self-medicating for the stress of high school. I knew that my new friends wouldn't sit across from me to have fake conversations just to ask me a question that makes me feel like ash. I looked at her, replied "great," and let her leave. This was the year I lost too many friends to count, and wrote too many essays to care.

Breathe it out.

The summer my brother spent in northern Michigan, roughly three hours from me, was hard. He had already been away at boarding school from August through June, but not having him around for summer was going to be new for me. My brother and I were the closest of friends when we were little, always having each other to tell secrets to, never being the tattle-tale that told Mom and Dad when one of us drew on the walls, or broke a chair. Then we got older. As school got harder for Scott due to his dyslexia, he began to look outward for security. The words he read and the moments he lived became a jumbled mess inside of his tired mind. When he found no outside relief, he would look down upon himself. He started to see me as his innocent little sister, stopped sharing his secrets, stopped being my best friend. Maybe it was that he didn't want me to worry about him. He needed someone who knew him as well as I did, but who could relate on a different level.

I went to the house that he was sharing with his best friend Chaz on Lake Leelanau that summer. When I got there, Chaz was sitting on the couch; Scott had just gotten in the shower. While we were sitting he asked if I smoked. I replied yes and he began to roll a joint. We told stories about our first time, asked which cartoon character we would love to smoke down the most, and of course, discussed the "new dank strain" he just got. The conversation that is usually lacked and lulled with Chaz seemed to roll. Scott walked out of the shower fifteen minutes later, his face broken into a dumbfounded smile. He sat with us on the worn out woolen couch and we lit the reefer. As we passed the joint, I felt a connection again. There seems to be a sense of community among marijuana users, a feeling of openness and acceptance that you don't always get with others. Scott sat and observed me, captivated by his own surprise. It finally seemed for the first time I felt like smoking made me older, not younger. "Mom and Dad would be pissed if they saw us," he laughed. In that moment it wasn't about them. It was about recreating a bridge with my brother. Since that moment, Scott has been able to share his secrets with me once again. He no longer sees me as his innocent little sister. We share our vulnerability and our strengths through puffs of unconsolidated snapshots of a smoky past.

Breathe it in.

A few weeks ago over winter break my brother, sister and I were sitting across from my parents at dinner. The conversation, as always, was light hearted and full of humor. My brother asked my parents if they had ever smoked weed before. My mom's cheeks tightened as she tried to hold back a forbidden smile. Eventually she nodded as she let her eyes drift back into the sea of nostalgia of her younger years. My dad's eyebrows rose to his receding hairline, taken back by the question and replied "Of course not." Mom's eyes shifted to him. She gave him the disappointed mother look that she has been practicing for the past two decades. "I thought I've seen you smoke before, but maybe it was someone else," she said disconcertingly to him. We all stared at him for a while, trying to replicate the face of my mother. Finally he broke the silence by saying, "Just promise me you guys will stop when you could lose something from it."

My mind races back to middle school, me sitting on my bed reading *Seventeen Magazine.* The headline of an article was entitled "Marijuana— the drug that makes you dumb, fat and ugly." I know the consequences of the drug, the gross exaggerations that could eventually fail me. I would hate to lose a job because I failed a drug test or lose a love because of a bit of weed. My brother, sister and I agreed to my father's request and later that night, as we passed a pipe outside, my sister whispered, "I love you guys. I am so glad to be able to have you with me for so much of my life," and as we went around, sharing each other's energy—the moment seemed to go on forever. Every second elongated. This feeling of euphoria from unconditional love, white winter snow beneath my feet, and hushed voices that warm my body.

That feeling—*I'll hold it in.*

Normality is Relative

By: Arthur Francis

> *"I was stuck between an extraterrestrial excuse and a terrestrial reality: alien origins were something I just couldn't accept, but my origins were too alien to accept normality."*

"We're aliens, you know." He was referring to himself, my brother, and I. "We're not from here. We're from another place." My dad brought that up every now and then if we were ever having some intellectual talk or questioning the world around us. I never really believed him, at least not literally. But I understood where he was coming from. I always did feel different from my peers and what the world held as the average. It was like some innate fact that I couldn't describe or place but yearned for; I demanded something I could point at and declare, "That's me. That's why I am the way I am." My family was just so different from the image of a "normal" family.

I was raised by my dad, who treated that title like a profession, and he was deserving of CEO, Chairman, and the entire board of Family Inc. He was so overqualified. My brother and I barely looked alike beyond our nose and brow, and our personalities had no concrete similarities. My mom was the furthest from any caricature of a mother's role or image. And this kind of helped – the concept of not being from "here." It was easy and it fit. But it separated me from my friends and the people around me. It separated me from humanity as a whole, even the entire world if taken absolutely literally, and my double helix structure prevented me from believing that. I was stuck between an extraterrestrial excuse and a terrestrial reality: alien origins were something I just couldn't accept, but my origins were too alien to accept normality.

My mother, Alice-now-legally-known-as-Hathor, is a beautiful 5'7 woman with a tranquil atmosphere and disposition. Blonde hair parted down the middle frames her high cheekbones. A radiant smile draws her cheeks taught and overcomes her eyes, a façade to the turmoil within her heart. A shadow of decay stalks her right front tooth, providing the only blemish on her joyous pretense. She is the eye of the storm, staying cadaverously serene within a maelstrom of credit cards, missed appointments, and optimistic plans for Hawaii and San Francisco swirling around her.

My mom has a past more convoluted than Anthony Weiner's moral compass. She was raised in El Paso, Texas, treated with electroshock therapy at twelve years old, married and enrolled in college at fifteen, and had three children before meeting my father — two from her first husband which she kept and one with another man that she had to give up for adoption — and throughout at least my life she has battled a meth addiction and a bipolar disorder. My father divorced her when I was three, and her scenes in my life have fluctuated since. She would be consistent for a week or two, holding arrangements relatively well and maintaining daily contact, but then fall off for a couple of weeks; and no matter what, the one constant was her inability to arrive on time anywhere. But she always has and always will be my mother, whom I love unconditionally. My brother, however, was not as lucky with our mother.

Endowed with a blonde crown and sapphire irises, David was born with a Divine Right to the opposite sex. His frame of broad shoulders and lean muscle kept him within one inch of me throughout our growth and elicited the proclamation, "Your brother is *hot*" throughout our high school tenure. His boyish charm and innocent smile has retained its youth well enough for him to monopolize the neighborhood lemonade stand industry and conceals his cunningly lazy mind that calculates the path of least resistance as effective and natural as water. An extrovert at heart with the semblance of a work phobia, he would sacrifice scholastic success if it allowed him even the shortest social outing. He was unlucky enough to be the younger brother who was just old enough to get grouped into everything I did at my age appropriate time.

My brother's past is building to be as disparate as Eliot Spitzer's sex life. He was taken hostage by marijuana and alcohol in high school. The standing theory for this is that he was the primary spectator to my mother's drug use and the consequent police intervention, and that trauma left more scars on him than me. At eighteen years old, my brother had been in juvenile hall for an assault on my father and me, earned a DUI while losing a chicken fight with my dad's van versus a light post, still has yet to technically graduate high school, and this past summer he displayed symptoms of bipolar disorder which actually ended up being a meth-induced insanity, as far as my father and I can deduce. My brother is lucky he was born to a father as strong and understanding as ours. He has supported my brother through his entire quest for answers, doing his best to fend off the flying monkeys and keep him on the yellow brick road. Our father is the main reason my brother still has a chance at a happy life.

When it came to my brother and I, my dad was a laborphiliac of Atlas proportions, wielding leadership as Alexander would Excalibur: with unwavering courage and diligent responsibility. Weighing in at a stout 250 pounds and occupying 6'3" of vertical space, my Father the Great is a misanthropic giant.

And yet, he has a past about as complex as Bill Clinton's marriage. He was raised in Los Angeles, California as the youngest of five children, yet he is the sole child to his father. His half-siblings were far older than he, the oldest being eighteen when he was born. Two of his sisters were pregnant by sixteen and one of them is now a grandmother with a grandchild older than me. Growing up, my father had bouts of alcoholism. He actually met my mother at an AA poker game, but he always drank non-alcoholic beer around me until I was about sixteen years old. He raised us in a pretty non-traditional household -- not just with him being a single dad, but also with how he interacted with us. He treated us as complete equals and only played the role of a father when necessary. Even now he considers us best friends more than father and son; and we gratuitously give one another the middle finger, always accompanied with a laugh and an "I love you bitch." But he sees himself in my brother. This last summer marks the second time my dad has been forced to watch meth claim someone he loves. His well of strength for dealing with my brother and I comes from his own past, when he too made similar mistakes.

Now—me. My past is about as complicated as three obscure political similes. I actually don't remember much of my childhood. If you asked Freud he might call this repression and a defense mechanism

I used to spare myself pain. And he might be right. But I don't really care what that cokehead has to say. To me, I was just lucky enough to be the older brother who started kindergarten early and didn't have to serve as the audience to my mother's tragedy. I was thirteen when I choked down my first ounce of whisky and just fourteen and a half the first time I inhaled marijuana fumes; but I never let myself become absorbed in these substances. I think my sense of loyalty to my parents is what kept me aligned. I had a very powerful sense of guilt since a young age, and that kept my dances with Mary Jane few and far between. I was the stereotypically successful son, for the most part; I respected my dad infinitely, I did well in school, and I played lacrosse pretty well. I still got myself into trouble though – I've been in cuffs twice and the back of a squad car once, but never in jail. Every time I see a black and white car, the one thing I remember is how they have slots in the back made for cuffed hands. It's funny to see what sticks with you after that kind of stuff happens.

But for the most part, I'm a normal guy. Looking at me, you wouldn't be able to see the path that winds behind my present point. You wouldn't see my meth-imprisoned mother. You wouldn't see my lost brother. You wouldn't see my troubled father. You would just see me, a good Cal Poly student with a 3.29 GPA and all the opportunity in the world. And that's all I would want you to see, because to judge me on anything else other than my present situation would cast me in a different light than I see myself.

So why this sense of separation? Why this feeling of difference, this yearning for some formal scapegoat? I didn't fit in with my family, but I didn't fit in outside of them either. In the frame of my convoluted, disparate, and complex identity of my formers, I'm an anomaly; in the frame of my ordinary peers, I'm an aberration. We were a family that would joke about my mom actually being on time for once (it was in the summer of '08), debate Existentialism and the philosophies of Kant and Pirsig, and remark on how Hitler probably felt as right about his actions as Ghandi did. I understood that my parents being divorced made me different. I understood that my mom's history and my dad's history made me different. I understood I was intelligent enough to understand all of this – but none of it made me any different. I was normal. I functioned fine. Freud can take his psychoanalysis and snort it up his nose. It's not my past that defines me. I inevitably define myself.

So, my brother may have his troubles, but he is socially outstanding and has a great sense of humor. Yes, my mom may have her vices, but she is the most caring and loving woman I've ever known. And my dad may carry the world on his shoulders, but he is honorable and honest and remains steadfast, no matter what relentless force acts on him. My upbringing has made me a dynamic character in my own story, and has shown me the complexity one life can have. It has given me a pliable sense of humor and an incredibly adaptable disposition. It has given me an opportunity most don't have—a chance to see the demons coming and steer clear of them before they can strike. I consider myself lucky for being granted the stage on which I could see the many directions a life can take.

With this particular background, I can answer my question: Are we really all aliens? Not literally (most likely). In fact, our similarities greatly outnumber our differences. Normality depends on the reference frame. We all have our own story and entangled past that make up our personal template, but how we use that template comes down to our own decisions. How will you use yours?

Record, Replay, Realize

By: Jennifer Haskett

"*I am breaking the shackles my mind holds me to.*"

Distinctive flashbacks to my youth. Repeat my tumultuous experiences where happy and sad memories intertwine. They claim my full attention and my mind fights back. I cannot fully escape them, and at times I wish I could be stronger. I search my thoughts to find the essence of who I am. My stream of consciousness is a movie in my mind.

Push play. My bulletproof façade shines to mirror the sun. It is another typical day, another chance to act one specific way, and to be perceived a certain way. "Look left then right. Chin up. Smile. Say this. Listen here. Play along." I repeat these mantras inside and glance at my reflection only to see a total stranger mimicking my moves. She grins. Today was tolerable, so she robotically praises herself. Despite the heavy burden on her already poor posture—this seems important.

"You are so lucky," chimes a nameless face looking at my too long display of dusty trophies that line my barren room walls. Beneath them lay my worn out cleats to rest. "Why can't I have your mind," recites another while inspecting my award ribbons. "I want your family," imparts one more staring at my mother's too neat display of family photos with that familiar girl trapped between two preferable brothers, enclosed by mom and dad, yet feeling secured by no one. This is not how I want to live; I have not always been this immersed in my head.

Push rewind. I am eleven years old at Northridge Park outdoor courts near Los Angeles. I look down to my basketball shorts, Big Dog t-shirt, and too long white knee-high socks mirroring my boy-cut hair, yet contrasting my awkward preteen body. I breathe in a smile full of light-hearted joy—an innocence untainted. I catch my breath. Sweat drips down my temple and seeps into my hazel eyes which I wipe away, unbothered. I look up and smile a smile that at the time was so familiar. My two older brothers stare at me, dumbstruck. They rightfully know I beat them at their own game of twenty-one. I am on top of the world, untouched and alive. I am in the moment.

Push fast-forward. I walk with desperate hope to the mailbox. I am seventeen. It is April of senior year, the air filled with laziness. My brown hair reflects tints of orange in the sun as my pale, freckled covering disagrees. I close the distance as I have the past twenty-three days with strong conviction that today will be the day. I turn down my favorite Florence + the Machine mix on my iPod. I close my wishful eyes and open the lid with desperate ease, so many anxious envelopes. I hurl bills and ads to the floor like mere shells compared to the precious pearl I need. And there it is, the metallic University of Washington

Seattle stamp. I savagely tear through it to reveal their congratulations. My heart beats once again. My dream school approves of me and within one month I accepted their offer. There is no aside nor continuous mental mapping. I am in the moment.

Push pause. These two memories flash through my head whenever my thoughts become overwhelming because at the time I thought nothing. I only felt the freeing exhilaration of being in the moment. The trouble is in my head; I see ordinary circumstances as unmanageable. Like others, my mind can deceive me at times. To get past this, I must live in the moment and not the fictional reality of my mind.

Turn DVD over and push play. Four weeks have passed and I am still seventeen, yet circumstances have taken a turn for the worse. I am now going on six straight days of not talking to anyone in my house. My brothers are both gone for college, and my parents told me I am not going to Seattle for college. I repeat. I am not going to my dream school for reasons I still have not begun to understand. The words resonate within the constraining walls of my mind. I am left behind and alone with my thoughts. I have never been this angry or hurt; my teeth chatter and stomach sinks. I have never felt so betrayed or unprotected; my heart aches and insides open. I have never felt this raw, myself on display. I never want to feel this again, so I am taking my final stand. I refuse to make this a recurring pattern.

These dismal thoughts are not beneficial. I cannot live my life in these constraints. This hurt and this anguish are not my parents' fault; they are mine alone. I can choose to take responsibility and to look ahead, not back. I get to choose not to sit on the sidelines because this has gone on for too long. I have realized that happiness is not a single destination. I refuse to give in, so it is time to get out of my head.

Skip a couple scenes. Two crucial months of improvement have passed and now I am eighteen. I wake up one restless morning and decide out of nowhere to take a risk. I jump out of bed, get in my car, and pull up to a place I never imagined myself. I am standing in front of Nathan's Tattoo and Piercing Parlor. Peering through the glass window, I see needles and jewelry. Yet, what I really notice is that my head is not as jumbled— not the usual hundred thoughts a minute. I did not overanalyze, worry, stress or debate; I just drove and ended up here. Now all that was left to do was press my cold, anxious hands to the railing that read, "Open." Twenty minutes later I parade out with a rook piercing. Unlike most, this piercing resides on the inner part of the ear. I chose this because its purpose is for me alone, not anyone else. The piece of jewelry reveals a hook—a hook for my life to come. It is a fresh start because no one knows the words that will follow, and no one knows the path I will take. This tiny piece of hand-beaded metal serves two vital functions. First, it temporarily pissed my parents off, but more importantly it took me outside of my chaotic head. My eyes are finally open. I am breaking the shackles my mind holds me to.

With this brand new outlook also came a huge surprise. Little did I know it, but my parents were actually capable of compromise. Cal Poly San Luis Obispo was just that. It became too difficult to dislike the friendly, caring atmosphere, to frown at the smiling passerbyers, and to despise this amazing university. Not everyone is fortunate enough to have this opportunity. I refuse to play the victim. My different perspective has allowed me to reach this new appreciation. I used to wish everything here was easier to hate so that I could stay mad at my parents. However, easy is not synonymous with college, nor is it with my life. My inner thoughts are a daily struggle to contain, but I have been practicing. I know it will get easier with time as it already has.

Skip to today. I am nineteen. I used to live inside my head, a lonely world with no visitors. My vision was obscured by my rampant thoughts, but now I am seeing more clearly. My confidence slipped away while I was questioning myself, but now I am grasping on to my individuality. My reality became tangled with lies from my own head, but now I am more careful. Love was given by family and friends but never received. I did not think I deserved it, but now I am finally accepting. I am still not fully there yet, but I am trying. I am aware.

I am an actual person: one human being. I cannot be everything at once. I cannot please everyone at the same time. But for the first time in my life, *I* need to be pleased with myself. I am alive and no longer just my stream of consciousness. I cannot explain my eccentric, misconstrued thoughts just like viewers do not always understand the movie they are watching. It may take two or three times to know the story just like it takes awhile for people to get to know me and understand where I come from. However, I am not a battery-operated, inorganic machine. I do not always do what people want me to, and I do not live my life by a script. DVDs' storylines do not change. I do. No one can predict my ending. I am more than my freckled-face and frequent awkward moments. Strangers everyday just see me as a nameless silhouette, but what I see ahead is a sky full of unpredictable weather, air full of endless possibilities, and the never-ending depths of hope. I know that I cannot change my past nor predict my future because I cannot control everything. I have to leave it be because that way I am present; I have my hook. *Push start.* Awaken.

The Final Stage of Healing

By: Jillian Elisberg

> *"Depression is an inescapable pit; I fell in it, tripping*
> *on the massive disconnect between my mind and body."*

The two looked out-of-place sitting in the cartoon-animal themed room.

Her mom perched on the edge of a miniature cow-spotted chair. Her

eyes were super glued to the pink giraffe decorated door. The young

woman was chattering and gesticulating with childish energy. The

doctor threw open the door and entered. For a few fleeting seconds, the

waiting room scene was at center stage, filled with impatient parents

scowling at the floor and scared kids. The door shut. The spotlight was

on the girl. The room's mood changed. She was silenced by a mask of

heavy, tense air. The neon giraffe watched, wide-eyed. The surgeon

muttered on. It was a silent film; the villain traced a line across the

girl's throat, saying "I'm going to get you." Her mom's hand flew to

her mouth, and her eyes raced laps around the room, looking for some

kind of comic relief. Her daughter, such a character, giggled again like

nothing had happened. Her eyes seemed to plead with her mom to stop

freaking out. The man left without another word. Finally, sound was

restored to the scene. Her mom looked distracted, missing the girl's

crucial question: should she bring her new black heels or would she

look like she was trying too hard if she broke them out for her first college party? She stopped and turned to me, her daughter, scheduled the next day for a surgery with a villain, and said "Jillian...You have cancer. Are you sure you still want to go to college?"

That night, my mind and body still felt like they were cleaved into two separate entities. My identity had started changing. I was whole, and now, thrown into a terrifying reality, my mind divorced my body for irreconcilable differences. My mom told my dad I was going in for surgery the next day to remove the *papillary thyroid carcinoma* that had taken root in my neck. He recoiled and shrank to the nearest chair. Again, I couldn't hear. It was a white out in my mind. Someone had cancer. Someone had to get a big surgery to remove their thyroid and some lymph nodes. That was sad, but it wasn't my life. I was going to go to college next week. My parents looked at me and asked if I was alright. Of course I was. I was going to college no matter what my dysfunctional body was up to. My mind wouldn't let my body force me to give up my dreams. I would not accept that my body had cancer.

A five hour surgery, ungodly amounts of *Hydromorphone* washed down with vegetable broth and two days in the hospital later, I finally got to go home. I caught the cancer girl's eye in my bathroom's mirror. She had grey skin and her chapped, pale lips were turned down on the sides. What really made her striking, though, was the horizontal slash in the middle of her throat. The two inch wide band of gooey blood was impossible to look away from. It looked like someone tried to behead the girl but didn't stick the knife in hard enough. I felt like I was watching a silent film again. But mirrors are honest, and I realized that I wasn't watching a movie but staring in morbid curiosity at myself. If I couldn't even look at my body without staring at my neck, what would everyone else think? This body didn't feel like it belonged to me anymore and I already knew that I would only be identifiable by a giant red slash on my throat. How could my body be the most honest representation of who I really am? I couldn't accept that the scar was a part of me, because accepting that would be accepting my cancerous body.

"I don't want to be the cancer girl," I said to my boyfriend.

"The right people will see through your appearance to the personality you've always had," he said.

"People are going to see my scar and nothing else," I said to my mother.

"You're in the middle of a battle with cancer and you're worried about the way you look?" she said.

"There's nothing special about me except for this scar, which makes me ugly," I said to my best friend.

"You're beautiful because you're unique. If people don't see that, screw 'em," she said.

I aggressively discounted their reassurances. I was still no closer to accepting this scarred body than before. I gave my body the silent treatment when I got to Cal Poly. My body wasn't a part of me— it just carried me. I didn't have to like it. I struck a ridiculous deal with my body: if I ignored it enough, it was only fair that everyone else would ignore it too. I wanted to disappear. Hundreds of people passed me every day and saw my scar. I was not a green-eyed, blonde-haired petite female. I was a walking scar. My mind felt irrelevant; my scar was the first thing people talked to me about. I could tell you about every single episode of *Good Eats*, the way swimming long distances makes me feel expansive, or Stephen Hawking's description of gravity using ball bearings. Unfortunately, on a college campus filled with thousands of strangers, what you see is what you get. I was my all-consuming scar. My body had betrayed me. I thought I had understood my body's purpose in high school. We read philosophical novels in English and Philosophy classes that led me to believe that I was a mind dwelling inside of a body, and the two had to get along for me to be the best version of myself. With my disobedient body, I couldn't figure out how to tie it back to my mind. My body was foreign to me.

One day in October, I was feeling particularly annoyed about my scar. I had woken up in the middle of the night to it stinging. A gross, bloody goo had oozed out of my scar and into my hair. I did not have time to deal with my failed body. I had to go to Chemistry. I slapped a bandage on and ignored it, and felt the now familiar stares of strangers on my way to class. I set my mind to pretending I didn't have a scar, maybe even for the rest of the day. But people don't let you forget. When I tried to buy an iced tea at the Ave, things went downhill.

"What's up with your neck?" the worker at the cash register asked. I paused. I went from calm to raging in a matter of seconds.

"I got in a gang fight. You should see the other guy," I said without blinking. There was a heavy pause.

"Oh…really? I'm…sorry? Here's your tea? Have a good day?" he questioned every statement now, confused and put off. And if I'm being honest, I, too, was confused and put off.

I know I'm not the only one who wrestles with body image issues. Loving and accepting your body is difficult, especially at this age and on this campus. I may have understood my body in high school, but I still went through my fair share of eating disorders and self-harm. My body was never good enough. It would become perfect through punishment and it needed to be punished over and over again because I was never perfect. I didn't know how to love my body, but I was on the right path. I've talked to girls who can't find a single thing about themselves that they like. I can't imagine hating everything about myself.

Accepting my body now is two-fold. I am once again that girl in high school, trying to gain confidence, but now I am also grieving the loss of my old identity. Just like I rejected my friends' and family's opinions, I dismissed what most of my therapists said as psychobabble. However, one of them somehow got through to me and introduced me to the five stages of grief. Denial and isolation? Check! I denied that this was my body. Anger? You got it. I hated my scar. I didn't want to exist in the failure of my body. Bargaining? Who in their right mind would make a deal with their body, hoping that my scar could escape the eyes of everyone? Me. Depression? Ding ding ding! We have a winner. I would spend hours hating myself, sobbing until I couldn't see out of my eyes anymore. Depression is an inescapable pit; I fell in it, tripping on the massive disconnect between my mind and body. Acceptance? I'm working on it. Acceptance could take years. I have to overcome my mind and be patient with my body. I can't accept my cancer until I accept my body, and the scars, again. Acceptance means stitching my mind and body up into one again, scars and all.

Breast, Noun

By: Eloise Armour

"Breast, noun: either one of the two soft parts on a woman's chest that produce milk when she has a baby."

For about six years now I've had large breasts. As of March 2012, I measured a 34F. Five sizes bigger than my mother, and three sizes larger than the national American average.

Over time my breasts have turned into a fleshy prison, an everyday burden: physically on my back and mentally on my self-esteem. It's a bittersweet realization. One would hope the cleavage would be a boost for my self-esteem, but instead I'm always worried about "it." I get anxious in the morning trying to figure out what shirt to wear and I don't run outdoors or do jumping jacks at the gym because of the attention it may attract. On the days when I decide to say "fuck it" and wear a more feminine shirt that may be slightly tighter, I might get some dirty looks from women, lewd comments from men, and blatant staring. Other tiring aspects of this heavy chested life occur at the Kennedy Library, where part of my job involves teaching courses about research for various classes. During some classes I feel like snapping. "This is not the fucking zoo," is what I tell students in my head as I keep on presenting databases and online archives. Other days I feel like crying. It makes me feel weak.

I am not known to be a shy person, not one to hide and have my breasts define who I am. But no matter how hard I try, they still define *part* of me. They affect how I run, how I dress, how I present myself to people, how I interpret interactions with people, and even how I sleep. I want people to know what it's like— the frustration, and the anger. I want people to understand that I always feel the need to hold down my breasts when I go down a flight of stairs, so they don't bounce obnoxiously. I want them to know that it can be painful to even just sleep on my stomach. I need people to know that at the end of the day, just a stare can feel like being stabbed. More upsetting episodes involve some of my close friends, who after drinking more alcohol than they should, would strategically corner me at parties to describe at length how much they fantasize and dream of my breasts. I wish I could say this was a pathetic, one-time accident, but it seems many men have similar reactions when they are drinking in the vicinity of my breasts. Regularly, I also get a sickening feeling in the pit of my stomach when I notice a male friend hugging me a bit tighter than he would have another girl, just to get a full feel of my breasts. It's not flattering; on the contrary, it's limiting. At times, it feels like my breasts have taken over my life; the color of my eyes, the skirt I have on, the joke I just said— none of it matters if my shirt is just slightly open. As if that is all I am to some people— that girl with the big tits. I feel othered, different. Men and women alike often only see me for my cleavage, shrinking my entire personality into a tiny box with the label "Has Big Boobs." Reduced to be considered for only one part of myself. Slowly but surely, it has changed my perception of men. I now often assume they introduce themselves to get better acquainted not with me as a whole, but my breasts.

Has this whole chestal ordeal made me a stronger person? No. There were no positive lessons to be learned, no growth in character and moral fiber. In the end, I've begun to resent what other girls call nature's gift to me, my best asset. In my day to day life, I avoid being serious about my breasts. I joke about them and try to make light of a situation I could only change with rather extensive and expensive surgery. I do wish I had better things to say about my breasts— a more positive note to bring in— but it's hard when every time I step outside, I feel like I need to conceal part of myself. It has been this way for as long as I can remember.

As a teenager having these boobs as my everyday companions was definitely harder, especially growing up in France. Catcalling and strangers hitting on women are more frequent throughout Europe; men don't hesitate to unceremoniously check out women, whereas they would be beat up for half of what they attempt if they were in America. More than soccer, catcalling is *the* European pastime. As a result, growing up in Paris made me resent not just older men, but the male population as a whole. I was an easy target for bored men, and an even easier one for those who saw how scared I was. The stares and comments became so obnoxious; I automatically translated the lust I saw in their eyes for aggression. This, accompanied by jealous teasing from less-endowed girls, was overwhelming. I quickly learned to change sidewalks when I would see a group of men ahead of me. I avoided going out without a scarf, but I never really learned to forgive the men who tried so hard to hit on someone who was clearly underage. This led, in part, to my 10th grade "rebellion" where I chopped my hair off in an attempt— in vain, to appear less feminine. I hoped the boy-short hair would make the breasts less important and make me be less of a target in a way. In the end this just fueled my anger even more as I realized these strangers were making me feel like I needed to change how I looked just to have the right to feel safe.

I wish I could change my attitude, be happier about my situation, or even change the way most men think about breasts. But it is tiring trying to explain why my 34F is hard to live with. Most people have a hard time relating, and understanding how suffocating it can be. I'm not sure what I'm trying to say with this essay; this isn't a rant against men, not an exasperated cry at catty girls, nor frustration with Victoria's Secret's limited sizes. Rather, I'm trying to explain that my breasts are *a part of me*, not all of me, or all of who I am. I wish it didn't mean so much to me, but there really isn't a day that goes by when I don't think of my breasts. It's exasperating to be judged by one aspect of my body— an aspect I don't even control. More than others, it's towards myself that I need to look for an answer. It does indeed make me angry to be judged, but I feel even more angry and heartbroken that I perceive myself to be judged so much. I've started to ask myself if others really do judge me as much as I thought. Do people really see me only for my breasts? Or are just the bad experiences, the vulgar comments, the staring that I've amalgamated in an ugly pile of negativity that skews my perception of others? Have I begun to misinterpret, and judge others the way I feel judged? I've realized that people may stare at my chest, but it doesn't have to change who I am. I don't have to cut my hair to hide, and I don't have to change sidewalks for others.

So what does all of this amount to? How does this better help you understand me as a person, as a human being? It doesn't. But it helps you understand what I am *not*: someone defined by my body. By acknowledging only my chest, people are missing out on what I love to do; how well I cook, the four languages I speak, the time I saw Eminem in concert, or how I kick ass kickboxing. People could be missing out on visiting me in Paris over the summer or my terrible jokes if they choose to remember me only as that girl with the big breasts. Although most people struggle to understand how this extra skin tissue and fat can be such a source of resentment and frustration, it doesn't mean they won't be able to understand me as a person. I've been told holding onto anger is like drinking poison and hoping the other person will die. It seems it may be time to toss that cup I've been holding onto.

Getting off the Lunge Line

By: Lindsey Holub

"*I am just not the type of girl who needs someone else to look after me.*"

When I first started riding horses at the ripe age of eight, I had no idea of the possibilities. The first few lessons I received were via lunge line. This is where the trainer holds a long rope to which the horse is attached; the horse will walk, trot and canter in a circle around the trainer. Starting on the lunge line is supposed to build a rider's strength and confidence without having to worry about controlling the horse. Let me tell you, I did not like the lunge line. I wanted to steer and control the horse by myself. I didn't want to be dependent on the trainer. I wanted to do it all myself. In life, it is sometimes best to ask for help and have a hand to hold, similar to the security of the lunge line. However, when all I wanted to learn to do was to stand on my own, similar to controlling a horse on my own, getting off the lunge line became my main goal.

The first step is getting off the lunge line.

I was fresh off the plane from a trip to my aunt and uncle's house when my family picked me up at the airport. Summer had come to an end and I was excited to start my fifth grade with my friends at Parkview Baptist Elementary School. I enjoyed my friends and the people there. It was comfortable knowing I had them to rely on. But my comfort was shattered on the ride home from the airport. My siblings and I had commenced our typical chit chat in the back seat when my mother announced she had some big news: "We are moving!" A moment of silence followed before my older sister threw her face into her hands and started to sob. Through her tears she managed to ask where we would be moving to. My mom replied, "I have decided to buy a home in the country a short drive outside of Baton Rouge. I am sick of the busy city life and I think it will be good for all of us to slow down for a while." As the car ride continued, my two younger siblings started to cry, probably because they copied everything my older sister did. I, however, remained silent and stared out the window. No friends, a new town, and no idea of how "country" life would be compared to the city life I had been accustomed to. The unknown can be overwhelming for a young girl, but I refused to let myself be upset over the move. I was determined to make the best of the change and be a better example for my younger sister and brother.

The first day of school came a few weeks later. I told my mom to let me walk in alone because I didn't want her to be there for me to hide behind. I muzzled up all of my fifth grader courage, held my head up, and walked into the school.

The next step is to learn the works of controlling a horse on your own.

Ever since I was very young, I knew that the one person I could always count on was myself. My mother is a chemical engineer by degree and currently runs the non-profit organization for a large chemical company. She is the type of person who knows the value of being an independent woman. She always said—with her nose pointed up proudly—that no one helped her get to where she was, and "sometimes life is hard, so you have to take out the trash." I don't know exactly what she meant by that phrase, but I assume it can be translated as "don't expect anyone to throw you a bone... do it yourself." My mother's influence pushed me to understand that if I want something, I have to be the one to make it happen. Because of her, I know that I am the sole person in control of my life. I rarely have to rely on someone else.

After that, it's time to learn to jump. A piece of advice...start small.

My middle school days were as awkward as anyone else's. I was coming into myself as a young lady and figuring out where I fit in. Then came the eighth grade graduation, which meant moving to high school the next year. Some people were afraid of the *jump* over, but I wasn't fazed by the move. I had two good friends at the time and I knew they needed me to be the leader. I was a very confident young lady by the end of eighth grade, and they were still figuring themselves out. I knew it was my job to make sure we would be okay in the "jungle" of West Feliciana High School. Although I cared about the well-being of these two girls, they would often annoy me with boy drama to which I would reply, "you're better off alone," and then mutter an "I told you so," when Billy or Jimmy broke one of their hearts. My independent attitude would often be mistaken for being "stuck-up." I faced a lot of scrutiny from other classmates for my unfriendly behavior. At the time, I remember struggling with my loner vibe. I wasn't the boyfriend type and would get annoyed when I was always the third or fifth wheel in a group of people. I decided it was time for a change.

Time to learn how to do a "lead change."

I recall a time when I decided I wanted a boyfriend. I was a freshman, and being the go-getter I am, I went for the hot senior. He was the typical tall, dark, and handsome type. His long, dark hair and pearly white teeth were a lethal combination for most girls, and I'll have to admit, even me. However, after a few dates where I was embarrassed by his manners and our "problem with communication"— and by problem, I mean he was dumber than a box of rocks— I broke it off soon after he asked me what the difference between caterpillars and worms was. All that relationship taught me was that I was right: you are better off alone.

Looking back, I remember how uncomfortable giving the lead to my boyfriend made me feel. I hated the idea of being dependent or needy and would get sick if I ever caught myself feeling the least bit reliant on him. I never understood why I had to wait for him to pick me up when I could simply drive myself to the movie. I am just not the type of girl who needs someone else to look after me.

It is now time to jump two jumps in a row, otherwise known as a complete line.

The summer before my junior year of high school—a huge obstacle in my eyes— I made a decision that greatly affected the course of my life. I decided I had no more need for high school. The petty drama I would hear the girls talking about, the classes that no longer challenged me…I just could not see the point in going. I did some research and had a few meetings with my counselor. I set myself up to graduate in three years. I would simply double my work and take junior and senior classes. The size of the work load was challenging, but I knew what was best for me. I also knew I had to start applying to colleges, so I could attend classes the following fall. I applied to a few universities close to home but none had the major I was most interested in: wine making. The closest college to my home state of Louisiana that offered this degree was in Colorado. After some research I decided that Colorado wasn't the best fit, so I looked to the one state that I knew would have the best programs in the business.

It's time to take all that you have learned and complete an entire course.

When I received my acceptance email from Cal Poly, I was elated. I couldn't believe I had gotten into my dream school. I didn't hesitate to confirm my spot in the class of 2016. After breaking the news to my family, they all offered their congratulations and said they would have expected nothing less. You might think that my family would struggle with the idea of me moving 2,000 miles away, especially at the age of seventeen, but they knew me well enough to know that nothing would stand in the way of me achieving my dreams of becoming a winemaker. My mother told me she was proud at the airport when she dropped me off. I gave her a huge hug and thanked her for making me so strong. Looking back now, I was never afraid to move to San Luis Obispo; although, I probably should have been, considering I didn't know anyone out here, and California is a different world from Louisiana. Thankfully, I met a nice girl who lived in my apartment complex with the same independent views as me, and we became good friends. By the time my first quarter ended, I had gotten into the groove of things and have never regretted my decision.

The only way to go from here is up. Raise the height of your jumps and continue to get better and better.

I love my independence. I often surprise myself with what I am capable of. I still have to pinch myself to remember I live in California. I think back to what my mother said to me: it is comforting knowing that I can rely on myself because at the end of the day, I'm the one person I am responsible for. As life goes on, I will continue to face each obstacle thrown at me with courage and determination. I hope to learn more about myself. I hope to inspire others to take things into their own hands and be less reliant on their friends and family. Who knows where I will end up, but there is only one way to find out—by getting off the lunge line.

The Gold Family

By: Katherine Seth

> **"...when my parents first separated, I was sure it was temporary. I had seen The Parent Trap I knew how this all worked."**

There were so many cracks on the ceiling that I was surprised it hadn't fallen in yet. Staring up at them in that small, stuffy room, I tried without success to ignore the film I was supposed to be watching. It was easier to look at the cracks. They stretched across the plastered ceiling of the city capital building like thin wobbly trace lines drawn by a giant, spider—webbing out from one corner of the room. One particularly long crack glanced down the wall, delicately halving Hawaii's state seal painted there. Our motto, "The spirit of the land is sustained through righteousness" seemed just a little less believable with an ugly crack slicing it in half. In front of me, an aging projector screen continued to relentlessly play its film about divorce.

The short film was called *The Purple Family*, and had allegedly won awards (I really don't know who decides these things), and the state requires all families filing for a divorce to watch it. My younger sister and I sat between my parents, a pattern replicated by other families throughout the rest of the darkened room, as if a seating chart had been issued prior to the film. On the aging projector screen set up at the front of the room, a mom dressed in blue and a dad dressed in red argued with each other, their hands thrown up in comical poses of frustration. Around them, the house that had began as purple at the beginning of the film now stood in varying degrees of dissociation, as if the paint had slowly separated into its two fundamental colors. Some rooms had accents of red and blue against a purple background, while other rooms were completely halved red and blue as if decorated by an indecisive painter. The film itself had the cheesy writing and bright colors reminiscent of the locally funded commercials I often saw on TV – Poncho's Solar, Kimo's Surf Shack, Zippy's – with everyone overacting and flashing shakas every 10 minutes. The childish simplicity of the film juxtaposed the tension that stretched between my parents like fractured glass. Every exaggerated eye roll or insult said onscreen felt like a light tap on the glass, and I waited for the one that would inevitably cause it to shatter. As I sat there, it all seemed like a garish and unnecessary experience to push on a family going through divorce.

In my sophomore year of high school, my parents contributed to the statistic that about 50% of married relationships in the U.S. end in divorce. I hated that. That fact isn't cited from anything. It has just become common knowledge at this point, cropping up in pseudo-serious conversations between high schoolers about love and its futility. Such an ugly statistic. I felt like it had swallowed up my parents too.

They had never really seemed to me like the "divorcing types," if that could be a type. To my child eyes, they mixed perfectly – my mother, full Chinese with soft hands and a soft voice, her temper slow like kindling, and my father, Caucasian and always sunburnt, funny and opinionated, with a temper that could shoot up unexpectedly like solar flares. Even their backstory was like a Lifetime movie – my mother's Chinese parents had initially disapproved of her relationship with my father, recommending she marry a "nice Chinese boy" instead. Eventually though, by eating more Chinese food than you would believe and learning to use chopsticks, he worked his way into their favor, proving that love truly can "bridge all things" – cue sappy violin strings and rolling credits.

Together, they created a childhood environment that was balanced and colorful, in which my sister and I languished unsuspectingly. We saw them laugh, go on dates, and every Thanksgiving they hosted a wine party. The sole purpose seemed to be to fill the refrigerator with pesto, wheels of brie cheese, and prosciutto, on which my sister and I snacked the whole night as we watched the adults get increasingly more giggly with each glass of Beaujolais they poured.

We were the family that always had dinner together, the four of us sitting around the dark brown wood of the dining table. My younger sister, Anna— taller than me and spouting Disney channel sass, yet occasionally making us privy to the compassion she inherited from our mother; me— perfectionist, awkward and introverted, but always the first to chatter away about my highs and lows at the dinner table; my mother— black hair cut short and neat, her smile warm and genuine, slyly getting us to share our stories; and my father— always the fount of knowledge, whether we wanted it or not, graciously bestowing his advice upon us. At the table, we shared our "highs and lows" of the day, a silly amalgamation of monumental test scores and incompetent coworkers. As a family, we were a unit, whole and healthy. When I reached the age when kids gathered into groups and complained about their parents and their family life, I found myself oddly quiet, having nothing to complain about myself, but eye-rolling along as if I too couldn't stand my mother or as if my dad as well just didn't "get" me. I felt perfectly at ease with my family. I leaned on them in a way I couldn't with anybody else.

That's why, when my parents separated in my sophomore year, I was sure it was temporary. I had seen *The Parent Trap*— I knew how this all worked. But when my dad left that one night in November, the zipper of his black duffel jingling against his leg as he walked away, he took the idea of "perfect family" with him. Suddenly, we were broken— all *hamajang* and messed up. We were simply a testament to the "unstable times we live in" and to the "lack of commitment that's crippling our nation". It took me a long time to begin telling my friends. I didn't want their pity. I didn't want them going home and telling their parents— who loved each other— what was happening to their friend Kat and wasn't it just a shame that no one stays together these days. Suddenly, I was "Kat, daughter of a broken home," and I hated it. My inner perfectionist cringed at our brokenness, watching my family break apart like pottery, the jagged pieces falling to the floor and cutting my hands. It hurt— hurt as if the chair I sat in at the dining room table, the chair I always thought was so sound, was to suddenly splinter beneath me into a million dark brown wooden pieces, sending me tumbling through nothingness. The family that I had leaned on my entire life was suddenly crumbling beneath me. I felt betrayed.

Sophomore and junior year marched on, and slowly, I let my parents' divorce swallow me up. No longer did I see myself as drum major of the marching band, or the girl who loves spicy *ahi* and poetry— I saw myself as that girl whose parents were splitting up. Poor thing, feel sorry for her, and whatever you do, don't say the D-word!

Looking in the mirror, I didn't see my long brown hair, highlighted by the Hawaiian sun, but instead, a dark haze that I kept draped around me like a shroud. Though my friends called my eyes "Rainbow Eyes" because of my bright hazel irises, the only thing I saw there was a turmoil that had never been there before, a fragility that kept me tiptoeing the edge of a breakdown.

Sometimes, though, I would forget about it all and life would feel normal again. I learned math and wrote papers and played my French horn. Then *BAM*— someone would say the D-word, and it would all come crashing back— the silence, the confusion, grabbing four plates to set the table for dinner and realizing, every night, again and again, that we only needed three. With a dry mouth and a hollow chest, I would put back the extra plate. Instead of defining myself by who I was, I defined myself by my circumstances.

It was under these circumstances that I got to see *The Purple Family*. Every month, state officials gather all families waiting for legal jurisdiction into the same small, stuffy room and show them the timeless story of a local Japanese-Hawaiian family grappling with domestic discontent. With a colorful cast of characters, such as Mother who is inherently blue, Father who is inherently red, Brother and Sister who are both sporting purple throughout the film, and Grandpa who is the old Japanese man who offers choice words of wisdom, the film "provides insight on difficult issues that arise when separation occurs" (Hawaii State Judiciary).

It has now been almost three years since my dad moved out, and "Kat, the daughter of a broken family," has slowly been buried, pushed away from the surface of my identity to the shadowy backstory. Report cards, yearbooks, prom photos, and college acceptance letters have slowly soothed the rawness of my parents' divorce, allowing me to define myself by who I am and not the "brokenness" of my family. Coming to college helped with this because I found other kids with "broken" families too, and I realized my family history did not isolate me. In an anonymous art gallery during orientation week, I saw a small piece of art that both shook me up and stilled me. Scanning the black shrouded wall of little white paper squares, my eyes immediately honed in on one. It said, "Though my family is broken, I am whole," in messy black scrawl over a pink heart, gold lines radiating outwards. Unexpectedly, I felt my throat tighten and my stomach clench, and I couldn't see through the sudden tears in my eyes. *Why is this happening? It's been years!* I quietly pushed my way out of the gallery, so I could let the tears spill down my cheeks, and let the sadness— or was it joy?— burst through the cracks I had spent years so laboriously patching up. Sitting there, with the gold San Luis sun filling up the trees, I knew then that I would not let my past keep me from this future I had chosen for myself. My brokenness is not something of which to be ashamed, nor is it my defining characteristic. It is a single aspect of myself, an aspect to be celebrated because it is one of the many pieces that makes me who I am.

Behind this word, "brokenness," hides a lot of misconception. It's as if what is not whole cannot be beautiful— that this state of "brokenness" is permanent and unchanging. Once something is broken, it can never again be as lovely as it had been when whole. However, experience and heartbreak have taught me that this is simply not true.

Recently, at an open gallery for architecture students, I learned the term *kintsugi*. It is the ancient Japanese art of repairing broken pottery with gold, the sole purpose of which is to understand that the piece is "more beautiful for having been broken." Yes, I am the daughter of a broken family, but there's a wholeness there as well. We are now the family that can talk about anything. Looking back, I realize that my childhood used to be full of silence. My parents would argue, not with words or shouting, but with silence. Since their divorce, that silence has been filled, our family meticulously glued back together by weekends spent at my dad's new apartment watching *Band of Brothers* and eating burgers, and evening nights cooking Chinese stir-fry with my mom in the kitchen. Though my dad no longer lives with us, I am closer to him than I have ever been before. Like taking a step back from a piece of art, the distance has helped me to see more of the man he truly is, rather than the man he thought he needed to be. I've learned that he loves to watercolor and is actually really good at photography. My mother is now a stronger woman than she ever was before, and daily she shows me how to be patient and compassionate, even when I've been hurt. That's true bravery. And me, the once perfectionist daughter— I am now able to see the beauty in imperfection. Like kintsugi, it is in the breaking and the mending that we realize our own unique beauty— through the cracks and the gold with which we fill them, we take on a luster unrivaled by perfection. Through the ordeal that was my parents' divorce, I now know the love connecting my family— a love that's been tested and strained— will not break, no matter the distance or the weight it bears.

Looking back now, I can't help but chuckle at the whole *Purple Family* experience. At the time, my fifteen year-old-self saw it as trivializing and stupid. Little did I realize then, but the childish simplicity of the film actually helped. Though it was a little overacted and silly, it's what we needed. We needed to know that this wasn't the end of all things. That, while it sucked and was awful, the problem could also be as simple as paint separating in its container. The paint wasn't broken. It wasn't somehow any less than what it had been before.

When the film ended, the lights came back up in the small room, and the tension between my parents seemed to ebb. My sister sitting next to me straightened up and yawned, the metal chair she sat on squeaking. Rubbing her eyes, she poked me and stuck her tongue out. Though I didn't notice it at the time, my mom's hand rested comfortingly on my shoulder. My dad ruffled my sister's hair. Little did we know, but slowly, quietly, our cracks were being filled. We were not purple, not blue or red, but gold, healing from the inside out.

Pockets Full of Sand

By: Greg Lane

> *"Everywhere I looked, I was being told, 'you are too damn weak.' That was something I needed to change."*

"Name and service," the man asked me, not looking up from his list.

"Gregory Lane," I replied. For the first time, I was allowed to put four words onto the end of my name, and I was not about to let anyone forget why I was here. "United States Marine Corps," I continued without hesitation. I moved down the hallway and took my first steps towards changing everything I had been and everything I would be.

Whenever someone would ask me, "Why the Marines?" my answer was simple. "People in the other branches of the military join to *serve* their country. Marines *fight* for their country." Since every person I talked to about enlisting asked me that question, that's about as complicated as I bothered to make it. I very well could have gone on a rant for a quarter of an hour, reciting endless bits of stuck-up arrogance about how the Marine Corps was the most elite of the military branches. But I didn't. I kept it short. I kept it simple. "But why enlist? Why not become an officer? You get treated better and get more money," they would always continue. "I'm not doing this for the money," would always be my reply. I never really told anyone why I was *really* enlisting.

My mother cried when I told her my plan. I do not like making my mom cry, but her feelings were not my highest concern when I did this. I did not enlist to make her happy, or my dad, my friends, or anyone else. I did this for myself. I enlisted to change myself. Being the youngest of three children is not exactly difficult. After all, I got to learn from the mistakes of my older brother and sister. However, the difficult part came in being the scrawny younger brother to a lifetime soccer player. Always better than me, faster, stronger, bigger — my brother, who is older than me by four years, was a shining example of how physically unimpressive I was. I weighed, as my friend Kevan always joked, "About ninety pounds, soaking wet and with pockets filled with sand." Throughout my entire life, I had always been uncoordinated, lightweight, skinny, not very athletic, and was never considered "strong." Because of this, I never felt significant enough. I was desperate for change, desperate for some sort of validation that I had a meaningful presence in life.

Through my entire life, I have never tipped the scale at more than 120 pounds, and that was on a very good day. And that was my problem: the scale. The one thing that always explicitly told me, "you are not good enough." Everywhere I looked, I was being told, "you are too damn weak." That was something I needed to change.

I never found a good reason explaining why, but when I registered for my freshmen classes in high school, I signed up for the Junior Reserve Officer Training Corps, a military based program designed to teach leadership and citizenship to high school students. At my school, the program was supported by the Marine Corps. Cadets were taught by retired Marines, given Marine Corps uniforms to wear, and males had to get proper, respectable haircuts. Higher ranking cadets were referred to as "Sir" or "Ma'am." The list of specific things we could and could not do went as far as cadets putting their hands in their pockets— a trivial, inconsequential action forbidden by my instructor— to thoroughly indoctrinate the cadets with as much of a military mindset as is politically correct for a high school. Even now, I will only raise my left hand to answer a question in class, for as my instructor declared, "raising your right hand means you want to get beat." Nobody questioned why this was; cadets just accepted his word like scripture.

Over the next four years, I was transformed into a magnificent beast of a cadet. I was known throughout the program for my impeccable uniforms and perfect knowledge. I was the Unarmed Drill Team Commander as a junior and the Company Commanding Officer as a senior, second in authority only to the instructors themselves. I wore a perfect high-and-tight haircut because it made me look "bad" and looked forward to Fridays because that was the day we wore our uniforms to school. For the first time in my life, I was incredibly good at something. The success I found in JROTC both established and confirmed my belief that the Marine Corps was exactly what I needed and wanted for the rest of my life. Nothing else.

As I walked single-file with the other military hopeful's before my senior year of high school, I knew exactly why I was there. I had made a promise to myself that I would change who I was, and enlisting would do exactly that. I was fed up and pissed off at the skeleton on the other side of the mirror. The Marines would change that. First on the list for the day was the medical exam. Urinalysis, hearing test, vision test, blood test, full physical, examination of every joint, height and weight measurements, and the doctors demanded an explanation for every scar. I was five feet nine inches tall. I had to be 127 pounds to go to basic training. To sign my contract and enlist, I had to be within 10% of that, or 115 pounds. I nervously took a drink of water before going into the room with the scale. There was no way in hell I was going to get disqualified because a scale said I was too skinny. "One-one-seven," the man rattled off before handing me back my medical record. By two pounds, I had made it. At the end was the final inspection. The doctor would take a look over my entire medical record to see if there was any reason I should be disqualified. The doctor who gave me my inspection was even awarded as one of the top doctors in the entire military for disqualifying people. After a few brief seconds of looking over my paperwork, he signed his name, handed it back to me and even said, "Congratulations." Now the hard part was over. I had beaten the scale. The only thing left was to not crack under pressure from a human lie detector.

"Get out of my da'gun office," the Gunnery Sergeant said to me when he first saw me. "I didn't tell you to come in here." I had walked into his office after my medical examination, like I had been told, with my brand new service record in hand.

"Aye aye, Gunnery Sergeant," was my reply. I quickly backtracked across the room and stood outside the door, feet on the threshold.

"Now get in here," he told me.

"Aye aye, Gunnery Sergeant," was my reply.

"I am here to make sure you don't try to lie, cheat, or steal your way into my Marine Corps. You understand that?"

Easily six foot two and twice my weight, this man in khaki now held my future as a Marine in his hands. I had aced the aptitude test, passed the medical exam, and now the answers I gave this man would decide whether or not I would be allowed to enlist. I stood by his desk as he asked me questions about the information written in my service record. He asked if I had ever had any broken bones, police involvement, drug use, and if I was on track to graduate high school the following June, among other things. If my answers did not exactly correlate to what was on my paper, I was a liar— and therefore disqualified.

A few days later, on the first of September, 2011, I took an oath to defend my country. No longer would I be looked upon as a "boy." Through blood and sweat (*not* tears), I would earn my place in this world. I signed where the man in khaki told me to, and the next eight years of my life now belonged to the United States Marine Corps. The next summer, my friends would be enjoying the sunshine, swimming in lakes, seeing movies, doing things teenagers do after they graduate from high school. I would spend my summer learning hand-to-hand combat, rifle marksmanship, small unit tactics— things men do when they prepare for war. I also selected and was guaranteed the most respected and esteemed job in the Marines: combat infantry. That part always confused people the most. Why would a kid who got a 2020 on the SATs enlist in the Marines and go into the infantry, of all things?

After all, I could do anything I wanted to in life. Therein lies part of the reason: I could do *anything* I wanted, and this was what I wanted. To hell with what the scale told me. I knew that if there was one place that would change everything about me, the Corps was it. The Corps would take the scrawny boy that I was and spit out either a man or a corpse. Semper Fi, do or die.

Just over a month later, a doctor sticks his head into the exam room where my mom and I are waiting. "Have you ever heard of a 'collapsed lung'?" he asks. My eyes dropped to the floor, and I felt my mom's eyes on me. The same thing happened to my dad while he was in college and my older brother during his senior year of high school, four years prior to mine. I was just carrying on the family tradition. *Spontaneous Pneumothorax*: the inexplicable loss of negative pressure in one side of the chest cavity, causing the lung to detach from the chest wall. All the doctor could say was that it happens to tall, thin males between the ages of eighteen and twenty-four. So yeah, I guess you could say we had heard of it. A few nights in the hospital and a tube into my chest later, I was all better— but not in the eyes of the Corps. Just before Christmas Eve, my recruiter called me and told me that I was medically disqualified until October of 2013. One hell of a Christmas present. The best option I had left for my near future was Cal

Poly. It certainly was not my first choice, but it was a decent back up plan.

Two additional collapsed lungs later, and I sit in my dorm room, typing about the single proudest and most disappointing event of my life. Now my hair is the longest it has been in the past five years. Gone are the buzz cuts, gone are the uniforms. However, nothing I wear can cover up the jagged lines of off-color flesh, the five holes in my chest. No feeling is greater than the pain of my lung being seared to my chest wall, except the feeling of failure for being too weak. No amount of time spent in the hospital can nullify the oath I took to defend my country.

I am by no means the same person I was when I began high school. Being involved with JROTC for four years fundamentally changed who I was, but whenever I look in the mirror, I still see skin and bones tediously set on a frame that is struggling to not collapse under its own weight. The skinny, underweight perceptions I developed of myself as a child still haunt me. The scarlet and gold flag on my wall and the camouflage backpack by my bed, once proud symbols of what I was doing with my life, now sit as dated, anachronistic reminders of who I once was. Although every tedious day of classes and homework brings me closer to a career in engineering and further from a future as a

Marine, I still need to change myself. Whether it be through enlisting or not, I have to change from the small, scrawny, insignificant person I am. That much I know for sure. That will never change.

Not My Clay Doll

By: Kiana Chan

> *"Through my search for my identity, I have learned*
> *that neither my appearance nor my ethnicity*
> *classifies me. In my future travels, I will carry pieces*
> *of both of my parents that will distinguish who I am.*
> *It will serve as a constant reminder that I am my*
> *mother's wanderlust. I am my father's practicality. I*
> *am truly their daughter."*

I plunged my pen-marked and glittery hands into the bag of cool, earthy clay and began sculpting the body of a girl. I started with her arms, legs, and neck. Then, I grabbed a sculpting tool— like one that a dentist would use to scrape plaque off my teeth. Gradually, I dug the fine tip of the needle into her face, drawing her delicate facial features. Brown eyes with a black dot hidden beneath the iris, a nose that wrinkled when she smiled, and a short black hair bob with blunt bangs. After blending colors and final touches to my clay avatar, I cautiously, but proudly tip toed across the classroom and set it on the table filled with the menagerie of my classmates' sculptures. All of the figures "wore" different colors for clothes, but I noticed that I was the only one in my class who used the color black for hair and tan for my face. What looked like a munchkin-sized, yet comparable representation of my outward appearance now looked awkwardly out of place amongst my class of mostly light skinned, light hair, and light-eyed first grade classmates. Although I felt out of place during school, once the school bells rang at 3:05pm, I would run out to the front of the school eagerly waiting for my dad's green Toyota Tundra. With my parents, I felt a sense of comfort knowing that I could be myself because they understood me. Maybe deep inside, I knew I was just like them.

"What are you?" This question makes me shrink a little bit inside. I think to myself; I am a person. I am a girl. I am a New Yorker. I am a Californian. The list goes on. I am Chinese. I am American. I am Kiana Chan. When I was younger, I usually grabbed the answer that I knew they were looking for: my ethnic background. "I am Chinese." But as I got older, I wanted to challenge the uneducated question that spewed from their mouths and the stereotypes that accompanied and misrepresented Chinese identity. Sometimes, I would tell them, "I am American." But that answer was never enough for my classmates or complete strangers who asked. Because of my outward Asian appearance, they would not be satisfied with my reply and would persist with the micro aggressive comment: "But what are you really?" As a child, I didn't know how to respond. I didn't understand the complexity of ethnic identity— and certainly neither did those who asked me. But now, I know that it's not my ethnic heritage that has shaped me. It has been the influences of my parents.

I am 5'5", and my long black hair falls over my shoulders like a mop. I awkwardly smile when I am nervous, and my cheeks turn bright red when I am embarrassed, caught off guard, or flattered. I enjoy wearing colorful, vibrant fabrics to represent my bright personality. I am eighteen years old, but I have the high-pitched voice of a child. When I stride, I swing one arm instead of two. I say hi to strangers. However, *I am* more than me. I am an individual embracing and struggling with what it means to be Chinese-American. After moving from southern Florida to the Bay Area, California when I was eight years old, I was shocked to be a part of a large population of Asian-Americans who, like me, all had black hair and brown eyes. And although we all have some intersecting experiences by sharing a common heritage, this identity has a distinct meaning to each one of us. When I was younger, my ethnic identity automatically made me unique from my peers. I believed that I was completely different from my parents. I felt that I had nothing in common with them. However, as I have become more independent and mature, I realize that their experiences and personalities have shaped who I am.

As a Chinese-American, I do not have a particular loyalty to either of these cultures. At home, Chinese culture is what our family makes of it. "Chi fan le! Yo, it's dinner time!" I hear my dad's attempt to speak Mandarin in his New York accent; his voice is loud like a fire alarm reverberating inside the house. His call rings with the cling clang of dishes, sizzling of stir-fried vegetables, and the mechanical song of our robot-like Zojirushi rice cooker. At home, we throw in Cantonese and Mandarin phrases here and there. We love the diverse dishes of Chinese cuisine. We remove shoes upon entering the house. I am Chinese-American in every sense of the word—a mix of cultures that is unique to my family.

The lively characteristics of my parents developed from their upbringing in the fast-paced and boisterous New York City, which built a distinct foundation for the rest of my family. Loud and dynamic, they stood out amongst the quaint stillness of Pleasant Hill, California, our home for thirteen years. My mother and father are polar opposites. Growing up, my dad told me stories about having his lunch money stolen in the schoolyard and pretending to only speak English so he could escape the Chinatown gang recruiters, getting into street fights on Mott Street after school with his classmates: Lemon Head, Monkey, Mongol, Bike Mike, and Toast. I grew up listening and laughing to his hilarious, interesting stories; but deep inside, I understood that it was not just fun and games for my dad: it was rough to live in the Lower East Side of Manhattan in the 1960's. My dad is strong and tall, arms and chest completely covered with symbolic tattoos representing our family: my mother's zodiac animal, the elegant and ferocious tiger roams through a bamboo forest. The Buddhist Goddess of Guan Yin sits on the right side of his chest, surrounded by intricate black clouds. My Chinese name, along with my younger brother's and older sister's, are imprinted on his arm. Despite his solid build, he throws tantrums when there is food left in the sink after a meal and never takes "No" as an answer. My father is big and muscular, but I can't help but see him as a loving, extra-large sized baby who likes designer hair products and shops at J-Crew. He cleans and he cooks. He likes to buy nice things. He is a baby in a grown man's body.

Although he grew up with very little money, his parents raised him like a prince within the walls of their New York City government-owned apartment. His mother laboriously peeled the delicate skins off of grapes for him to eat, and his father, a cook during World War II in Germany, fed him steak dinners. His parents showed their love for him through food. My parents had very different ways of displaying their affection for my siblings and me. While my mother would rather take us on long vacations to tropical, third-world countries, my father preferred to show his love toward his children through the random toys, clothes, or gadgets that he bought for us. Thrifty like my mother, I would often decline his bribes to buy me sequined Betsey Johnson dresses or Swarovski crystal necklaces. This frustrated him because he didn't understand why his daughter would reject such nice gifts, a privilege that he never had as a child. He would often warn me with an urgent undertone in his voice, "Kiana, I'm serious, don't let mom get into your head. God dammit, buy whatever you want!" Although I appreciate my father's intentions, I agree more with my mother: life experiences are more valuable than material things. With $2000, we would rather buy round-trip airline tickets to Nicaragua than have a Spring edition Marc Jacobs purse. It was hard for my father to accept the fact that we were different in our views towards material goods versus travel experiences.

Unlike my dad who obtains satisfaction from material goods, my mother lives for experiences. A luscious mane of hair, which she dyes with henna to disguise the aging grey, shimmers bright red in the sunlight. Although she was born when gas only cost fifty cents a gallon and when milkmen made the neighborhood milk deliveries, like Hebe, she has kept her youth and is often mistaken for one of her daughters from behind. She is free spirited and fun, yet assertive; she is unafraid to speak up if she disagrees with anything. Extremely extroverted, she befriends strangers in the park and on the New York City subway. Filled with wanderlust, she dropped out of college during her second year, and against her mother's will, she left everyone she knew and bought a one-way ticket to Greece. She travelled across Europe with no plan, no place to stay, and minimal cash. Undefined by the precepts of a conventional mother, she is daring and ambitious, haphazard and carefree. A vacation with my mom includes volunteering on a pineapple farm in the tropical heat of Costa Rica, disguising malaria pills in Guyabano smoothies, and battling oversized mosquitoes with homemade vinegar bug spray.

Through the memorable vacations with my mother, I learned the extent of her impetuous behavior, and also how similar I was to her and my father. During a vacation with just my older sister, Kaila, younger brother, Lucien, and mom, we stood hesitantly at the edge of the dock by Lake Atitlan, a vast, volcanic lake in the highlands of Guatemala. I saw my mother talking with a stranger in her nearly fluent Spanish. "Cuanto cuesta? How much?" she asked. Small in stature, with sun stained skin like leather, the man wore a disintegrating straw cowboy hat. He stood balanced on the edge of a deteriorating, sun-bleached rowboat tied loosely to the dock with a twine string. His mouth shaped into an algal grimacing smile and I could see his golden canine tooth glisten in the sunlight. My mother stepped onto the poorly crafted chunk of wood that sunk halfway under the weight of her body. Water crawled into the makeshift boat while she struggled to find her balance. Kaila, Lucien, and I stood wide-eyed with disbelief while we waited for our mom to barter our fate away with the ferryman from Hades. "Come on guys! Let's take this cute boat across the lake!" she persisted. I looked at Lucien, only seven at the time. In that moment, he wore his stubborn face with his pursed lips and wrinkled eyebrows, and Kaila, who was twelve, looked like she had just seen our grandmother's ghost. "Mom, no way!" I declared. I pointed towards the vast body of water, blanketed with pumice stones. After stubbornly remaining in the boat, she realized that she was outnumbered. Arms crossed in a teenage-like reluctance, she finally gave in. "Fine. Let's just be boring and walk around the lake instead."

At only ten years old, I had to be persistent and assertive with my mom because she was just *too* easygoing. Completely oblivious to the danger of the situation, she was willing to risk losing our passports in the depths of the lake, and then what would we do in Guatemala for a month with no clothes, no malaria pills, and no cash? Or what if we drowned? I felt like an ambassador to my siblings, protecting their lives from my adventure-craving mother. In that moment, I felt like my dad. When it came to potentially dangerous situations, my dad and I become very uptight and anxious. Our impatience and apprehension would not be cured until we resolved the situation. My mother always tells us both to "take a chill pill," attempting to heal our uneasiness.

Growing up, I felt like the dominating personalities of my parents suppressed the development of my own character. Throughout my childhood, I was convinced that I was nothing like my parents. Preoccupied with trying to define what my ethnic identity means to me and who I am, I often lost sight of what was right in front of me. Just like my mom, I am spontaneous, adventurous, and extroverted. I thrive when challenges come my way, and I take the opportunities that will help me develop as a person. I am daring just like my mom. I dare to flee the country and leave all of my ties behind, just like my mother did in the midst of her college years, because I yearn for changes in my life. To travel the world by myself is a dream that I've had ever since I was young, but this dream did not just stem from my imagination. I live vicariously through my mom's experiences travelling across rural Germany in a burnt orange, 1980's Volkswagen van, salsa dancing in Cuba with her Spanish teachers, climbing snow capped mountains in

China. Through her, I have fallen in love with places that I have never been to. I am full of wanderlust like my mom; we believe that escape will cure our discontent. I want to explore different countries, not only to immerse myself in new cultures and languages, but also to experience myself in different contexts. Although I am still discovering who I am, one thing I know for sure that I desire to travel. It is so hard for me to live in the present when I have so many visions, images, and experiences that I need to pursue during the timeframe of my life. When I travel, I feel free from the suffocating pressure that society has ingrained in me to define my ethnic identity and how it has shaped who I am. When I travel, I can be whoever I want to be.

But I am also just like my father. We are perceptive and observant. When he goes to restaurants, he sits in the chair that faces the door paranoid that someone with a gun could come in and start shooting. He always types his emails in CAPS LOCK because he thinks that everything he has to say is urgent. Incredibly cautious and very superstitious, he relies on timeless clichés to teach me life lessons. *The early bird catches the worm. Always look for an open door. You snooze you lose. Be the best of the best.* Despite our obvious differences, the similarities between my father and I have helped me learn more about myself. Our passion for cooking and food is only one thing that brings us together; through his actions and his personality, I have discovered parts of myself that are just like him.

In just a few years, I can imagine myself exploring the canals of Amsterdam, biking along its cobblestone paths, passing bright pastel homes and coffee shops with nothing but my wanderlust, my passport, and my memories from home. Or maybe I'll be cocooned in a frayed hammock on a wooden balcony, watching the rain pour down into the deep green Costa Rican rainforest; lost in thought about the distant memories of my childhood while sipping a warm, foamy cappuccino. Memories of my childhood like that of my clay doll: the one with black hair and brown eyes who felt so out of place among all of the other dolls. Where did she go? Is she lost forever?

This figure has been lost for years. What was once a representation of myself as a child, no longer has the same meaning. Through my search for my identity, I have learned that neither my appearance nor my ethnicity classifies *me*. In my future travels, I will carry pieces of both of my parents that will distinguish who *I am*. It will serve as a constant reminder that I am my mother's wanderlust. I am my father's practicality. I am truly their daughter.

A Dance with Myself

By: José Parra

> **"The vast majority of stupid or spontaneous things that I have done in my life can be explained in five words: It was for a girl."**

Tonight's going to suck, I thought to myself as the lights began to fade. I knew exactly what would happen next; after all, this is my least-favorite part. The lights go out and it's pitch black. *Oh no, here it comes.* Cheers travel across the room, each one begetting another like an extremely contagious, overexcited yawn. Light returns in technicolor, the massive speakers blast a wall of sound to the tune of "Suavemente" by Elvis Crespo, and bottles of Corona and Coke get friendly with the floor as the crowd (led by my parents) stampedes to the dance floor. The man behind the music brings a microphone to his lips…*"Damas y caballeros, ¡Que empieze la fiesta!"*[1]

There I was, at yet another cousin's quinceañera [2] in Puerto Rico, my butt steadily fastened to my chair, my parents dancing their hips out, cheering toward me in a clear attempt to embarrass me, while the rest of my family poked fun at me for not dancing. I was in my very own, tailor-made torture chamber. Picture *that guy* at the party who always has his back to the wall and an angry frown on his face: that was me. I *was* that guy, but not anymore. In fact, my parents aren't considered the dancers in the family anymore— I am.

For most of my life, both sides of my family knew me as "el amargado," or the grouch. That's a lot of ridicule, seeing as how my family consists of three grandparents, thirteen aunts and uncles, thirty-something cousins, and God knows how many "aunts" and "uncles" and "cousins". Honestly, I don't blame them. From the point of view of a traditional Mexican family, it is very strange for a teenager to dislike dancing since it is such an integral part of our culture. In my parents' day, dancing was the pinnacle of social activities; so, naturally, it is difficult for them to imagine dancing as something that might be embarrassing, which was the way that I viewed it. It was easy for me to understand why my family found it strange that I didn't like to dance, but for the life of me I could never understand why they enjoyed dancing so much! At parties everyone (but me, of course) would rush the dance floor and have a blast for *hours*. My parents, who cannot walk up a flight of stairs without stopping for breath, would suddenly be instilled with superhuman endurance. I just didn't get it.

"Dad, why did you guys dance so much back then?" I asked him one day at the dinner table. A smile crawled up his cheeks as he rolled up his napkin and placed it on his empty plate, "*Mijo [3]*, you have a girlfriend right?" he asked. "No!" I lied. *How did he know! I haven't even told anyone!* I thought. My smile began to match my father's. "You like to kiss her right? To hold her hand?" he said, ignoring my previous remark. I let out an awkward stutter; he burst out in rumbling laughter. "That's why, *Mijo*, because back in the day your mom and I couldn't *hold hands*. If your grandpa caught me even *looking* at your mom, he would have sent all of her brothers to give me a beating. The only time your mom and I could even touch each other was during the parties, when everyone was too drunk and happy to notice your mother and I dancing," my dad explained. "You mean, except for when you two would sneak out in the middle of the night. Right *Apá[4]*?" I teased. His smile widened even more, "How do you think I got these scars?" he chuckled while pointing at a cluster of faded blemishes on his cheek. Why on earth would my dad risk getting beat-up by my mom's six older brothers just for a dance? I still didn't get it. Then I met Beatriz Torres.

The vast majority of stupid or spontaneous things that I have done in my life can be explained in five words: It was for a girl. And learning to dance is no exception. Beatriz, or Bea as I called her, was a beautiful and talented soprano in my high school choir. Bea's dirty-blonde hair was curly and extremely voluminous; it felt like it took up more space than her entire body did. She was small, only about 5'2", but her personality, poise, and abundant curves awarded her more presence than another four feet would have. Her smile was always genuine and her gaze, confident. That girl knocked me out.

One day, a member of the choir invited everyone to a party she was hosting to celebrate the end of the year. I already knew I wasn't going to go. So when Bea walked up to me and exclaimed "José! You're going to the party right?" I answered with no hesitation, "Of course I am! I'll see you there!" And then there I was: my back to a wall and a frown on my face, but Bea came to my rescue. "Why aren't you dancing?" I asked her. "Well, no one really knows how to dance salsa here, so I'm taking a break," she explained. She rearranged her dress; it hugged her curves perfectly and matched her deep red lipstick.... Absolutely. Breathtaking. To this day, I have no idea what got into me. Maybe it was how gorgeous Bea looked, or maybe someone spiked the punch, but for some reason I said, "Really? I know salsa. Would you like to dance?" Bea's radiant smile revealed itself behind her rose-red lips and— to my horror— she grabbed hold of my hand and dragged me to the center of the room.

In the middle of the dance floor with a remarkably beautiful girl— I was petrified. "Well come on then, let's dance!" she said, placing one hand on my right shoulder and the other in my left hand, "You said you know salsa, right?" There was a pause. I panicked. I didn't know what to do. Suddenly, it came to me. "Oh, you misunderstood, Bea." I said, trying as hard as I could not to faint, "I said I know salsa, of course I know salsa. I'm Mexican! I can make you salsa any day of the week. But that was small talk; I just wanted to dance with you." There was an even longer pause. Years passed, my heart raced, and my brain screamed at me. *What are you saying? You're an idiot!* Suddenly, Bea nearly falls over laughing, leaning on my shoulder to stay upright. "That's a new one!" she sputtered, still laughing "You know what? I'll just show you. Sound good?" she said with a smile. *YES, YES, FREAKING HELL, YES, THAT SOUNDS GOOD!* "Yeah, sure," I replied. She showed me the correct posture, the basic step, how to spin, and before I knew it, I was dancing salsa, and I loved it.

After a couple of songs, Bea and I sat at a table and talked for awhile. I couldn't help but be mesmerized by her confidence, and I was surprised that she enjoyed my company. "¡*Mira! [5]* They're bringing in live musicians!" she exclaimed, "Well you know the steps now. Let's dance for real this time!" She looked straight into my eyes and grabbed my tie. Once again, she pulled me toward the dance floor, walking backward, never breaking eye contact. Our hands met, and fell in love.

We faced one another, her palm resting lightly on my shoulder; my fingers wrapped gently around the concave of her waist, a pose that felt like two puzzle pieces fitting into their places. *Tun-Tack!* The congas sang. My steps became a metronome— her hips, a pendulum. I kept the rhythm as she kept the time. *Tun-Tack!* Bea's elegant movements harmonized with every beat of the drums' song. I nudged her side, a proposal for the next step. She willingly accepted and together we changed positions, jumping a broom that isn't there. *Tun-Tak!* I raised our married hands above her head, and she twirled gracefully on the balls of her feet; I complemented her with a spin of my own, but our hands never divorced. By now, our romance had lasted through most of the song, but we had reached the final chorus and knew our time left together was short. As *el salsero*'s [6] voice began to crescendo we gave it our all, emptying ourselves into one last, passionate verse.

When the song ended and our hands finally parted, I was a new man. I had a new passion and confidence that branched to every aspect of my life. After that party, not only did I lose my animosity toward dancing, but I also gained the confidence to enjoy my youth for the first time. Now I have no qualms with spontaneous conversations with strangers, or with speaking my mind in public, and I'm the first to ask a girl to dance at a party. That dance was the farthest that I ever got with

Beatriz Torres, but I am thankful for our three-minute marriage. I believe that dancing with Bea sparked the beginning of the prime of my life, and, more importantly, helped me understand that like my parents, my prime never has to end.

Tonight's going to be great. The room was dimly lit and relaxing, and smelled sweet with rum and coffee. The guitarist finished up his last song with a beautiful arpeggiated chord, each note followed the last in rapid succession until the guitar rang with a clear and warm tone. The lights dimmed further, fueling my excitement, as the guitarist packed his instrument. Soon he was walking out the door. It was dark now. *Yes, here it comes.* I thought. All I could see was the moonlight coming through the window and reflecting off of the bottles of Bacardí and Don Q. I have been keeping my eye on the girl sipping coffee in the corner of the room all night. She moves gracefully. She definitely knows how to dance. I see a man pick up a microphone, and place his hand on the control panel for the stereo system. I know exactly what happens next; after all, this is my favorite part.

[1] "Ladies and gentlemen, let the party begin!"
[2] A traditional Mexican celebration commemorating a girl growing into a young woman, at the age of fifteen
[3] Spanish term of endearment, meaning "my son"
[4] Spanish term of endearment meaning "father"
[5] "Look!"
[6] Male salsa singer

Biographies

Arthur Francis

Howdy, y'all. I'm Arthur Francis. I'm a business major at Cal Poly and enjoy bareback horse riding, sunsets that really are pretty mediocre compared to the other ones I've seen, and misleading people with jokes. (I actually do love psychology, the studies of human behavior, and the nature of financial math.) This paper was something I, apparently, needed to get off my chest. The cool thing about time is everything makes sense in hindsight, yet rarely ever does in the present moment—and in the moment I kind of just threw this onto the page without thinking about it. I had to deliberately write out good qualities for each of my family members, and in doing so I got to challenge my initial perspective. And still, none of these simplified anecdotes do the reality justice. Attempts to tie down reality never do. The most telling part of this was noticing the things I didn't write down. It's hard to share something so close to me—to us. But getting it out lets us poke at our stories from new perspectives. This paper probably marked some internal transition. It probably served as some expulsion to unconsciously drive myself. But I won't know until tomorrow.

Brenna Weeks

I graduated from Art Center College of Design in Pasadena with a Bachelor of Fine Arts and currently reside in Los Angeles. Growing up in a divided household on the outskirts of Los Angeles, I got to see both ends of the workspace spectrum— my father, a photographer reveling in creativity, and my mother stuck in a corporate office from nine to five. At four years old, I decided that I would never want to waste my life as a corporate drone behind a desk. From a young age, I always had a camera in hand, going around the house capturing anything and everything— filling a memory card, deleting the contents of the card, then going out and shooting once again. To be able to collaborate, to create with other artists, to engage in the production process is what drives me. To create something magical enough to make someone stop and stare, and make an interpretation about my work— this is what keeps me creating. But the real reason why I subscribed to a job title with the word "starving" in front of it is that I cannot picture myself doing anything else. This is my dream job.

Eloise Armour

I am a French-American student who loves international politics, cheese, kickboxing, and avocadoes. The love of cheese comes from growing up in Paris, and the love of avocados comes from living for the past four years in California. My passion for international politics comes from living between the two. Moving to California for college has been eye-opening. I discovered a whole new way of life, a whole new way of being, and I absolutely cannot wait to see what is in store after graduating. Editing and being on the verge of publishing this essay two years after first writing it, has been an odd and interesting experience; it's as if a different version of 'me' had written it. Writing this essay my sophomore year of college allowed me to express a lot of feelings I had kept hidden, and it was the first step in making peace with my body. I no longer wish to have surgery. I truly hope others can see themselves in my piece, and perhaps accept themselves.

Erica Barrios

I was raised in the city of Downey, California; although, multiple and continuous moves have left me unable to distinguish a specific home base. I currently study Languages, and their coinciding cultures, at Cal Poly San Luis Obispo, with a minor in Women and Gender studies. I'd most easily summarize myself as a closet-writer, book-worm, feminist, and aspiring polyglot with a natural dislike for the attempt to boil myself down to one written paragraph. Somewhere between a conditional introvert and an unremitting over-thinker, I write passionately as a means of introspection. I hope my writing will eventually achieve meaningful value beyond myself. "All Things in Contact with the Sea" was a means of coming to terms with the events of my past. I explored the continuous tension between escape and presence as guiding forces throughout my life, and allowed them to maintain this pull in my writing as well. I forced myself to navigate that space between lyrical writing and a more conventional style: thus making this piece, in a way, the written coalescence between my strengths and weaknesses. I discovered a center union there and then… delicately balancing.

Greg Lane

"Pockets Full of Sand" is easily one of the most introspective pieces I've ever written. For the first time, I was truly challenged to take a good look at my past and analyze who I am now. I wrote this story in the fall of my freshmen year. Looking back, I realize how little connection there is between who I was in high school and who I am in college. I maintain most of the same interests, but my personality has shifted. The only thing relating that old version of me and this new one is the body that we share— and our views of it. That realization helped me find the themes of this piece: self-image and masculine constructs. Writing this piece has helped with my personal growth and allowed me to identify the few underlying things that are important. It may just be the different culture I am immersed in at Cal Poly. Back home in Snohomish, Washington, a small town just north of Seattle, I never really had purpose in life. But after two years studying mechanical engineering, I have found something that interests me and is worth doing with my life.

Jennifer Haskett

With "Record, Replay, Realize," I set out to write a piece that would give readers insight into my scattered mind. I used the metaphor of a DVD player as my stream of consciousness. I hope this unique approach keeps the reader's attention with its flashbacks and asides. My intent was not to be fluid or poetic; I simply wanted to be portrayed in a way that was true to myself. I ventured to transform my three-dimensional experience into words on a two-dimensional paper. This journey began with my move from the San Fernando Valley to San Luis Obispo for college where I soon fell in love with the friendly, small town atmosphere. Currently, I am working towards an undergraduate degree in business administration with a focus in accounting and a minor in psychology. Overall, I hope to not only achieve academic success, but to also continue figuring out who I am while navigating change. To do so, I must continue to be more than just my stream of consciousness.

Jillian Elisberg

Four surgeries, one mega-dose of radioactive iodine, and a promise to regularly get a scan to check for more tumors later, I am finally (hopefully) done. The words to describe how it felt to have cancer during my freshmen year of college were piling up in my head, threatening to spill out if I didn't acknowledge them. This was both the easiest and hardest piece I have written: I knew what I had to say, but admitting my feelings on paper made me feel everything again. I would love to say that by writing this, I found that ever-elusive acceptance. But, honestly, I'm still working on grieving. A friend recently shared with me some words to live by: "*piano, piano,*" an Italian phrase that roughly translates to "little by little, with intention and care." I'm getting better. I no longer feel like a walking scar. I am more than that. I am a nineteen year old sophomore at Cal Poly. I am a food science major with a minor in psychology. I am a Colorado native. I am a fighter. I am not a scar. I am not my cancer. I am Jillian.

José Parra
I grew up in a small town called Antioch in the East Bay, but I have had the privilege of living in many different places. Although most of my relocations were reluctant, I have grown to appreciate the experiences each place has awarded me. By far, my most significant and memorable move was to the island of Puerto Rico when I was fourteen years old, where this story takes place. The story of my dance with Bea was a defining moment of my experience in Puerto Rico, and I decided to write about it because it encompassed one of the most important lessons that I learned in my time on the island of enchantment— participate. Take risks. Dance.

Katherine Seth
Though I was born in Berkeley, California, my home is on the island of Oahu, Hawaii. Being an out-of-state college student in California, people often ask me what it was like growing up in "paradise" — followed by the question "Do you surf?" (I can… but not well). When asked this, I respond with what I know they're looking for. As a kid, my grandpa took me to get mango shaved ice after school. I learned that rubbing *naupaka* leaves in your snorkel goggles would keep them from fogging up. At my high school graduation, all the girls wore flower leis around their heads. But really, growing up in paradise is the same as growing up anywhere. I went to elementary school and learned I loved writing and reading. Middle school was a terrible time of braces and school dances. And in high school, I decided that I liked architecture enough to study it for the next five years. I have since fallen in love with architecture here at Cal Poly, and my dream is to one day build sustainable and affordable housing for needy communities all over the world. Though it was difficult to leave Hawaii, everyday I discover a little more paradise in San Luis Obispo: the warm people, the shockingly blue sky, and the rolling golden hills that go on forever. This is the perfect place to prepare for my future, and until then, I will keep writing, healing, and eating mango shaved ice. The future is golden, and I will be ready.

Kiana Chan
Surrounded by the loud, distinctive personalities of my parents within our small household, I am a product of them both— reflecting pieces of their characters that distinguish who I am. I wrote this piece to demonstrate my struggles with defining my ethnic identity, while weaving in my desire to travel the world as a means of discovering who I am. Through anecdotes from my childhood and future aspirations to

explore and travel, I have been able to identify that the main influences of my personality and aspirations lay in the very household where my family lives. This is a story of understanding and growth. Through writing, I have been able to discover more about who I am; however, the path that I would like to follow is still ambiguous. By going through new experiences and doing what I love most—traveling— I hope I can continue this process of self discovery as I approach adulthood.

Leslie St John
A native of Arkansas, Leslie St. John received her MFA from Purdue University, where she served as poetry editor for the Sycamore Review. She is author of *Beauty Like a Rope*, published by Word Palace Press, and her poems have appeared in various journals, including *Cimarron Review*, *Crab Orchard Review*, *Florida Review*, *Indiana Review*, *Linebreak*, *Oxford American*, *Pinch*, and *Verse Daily*. She won the MacGuffin Prize, judged by Thomas Lux, was runner-up for the Florida Review prize, and was nominated by Lisa Lewis and Ai for a Pushcart Prize. Mark Doty chose her poem, "Filling the Egg Carton" as a finalist for the Inkwell prize. Her most recent work appears in *Aperçus Quarterly*, where she was the featured poet. To view her poems and interview, "That Weaving is Liberation: A Conversation with Leslie St. John," visit the archives at www.apercusquarterly.com. As a dancer and yogi, she is interested in the intersections between the body, movement, and poetry; her most recent project is Prose and Poses, a yoga and creative writing workshop. She also teaches English at Cal Poly in San Luis Obispo, CA.

Lindsey Holub
I grew up in a small town in South Louisiana. The summers were long and hot, but the food was delicious, and the people were wholesome. When I was a sophomore attending West Feliciana High School, I realized what I wanted to do with my life: become a winemaker. My father, a chemical engineer, enjoyed making wine in our guest house and let me help. Making my very own batch of Cabernet Sauvignon hooked me. After applying to a number of schools that offered a wine-making program, I was accepted to—and fell in love with—Cal Poly. I picked up and moved to the Central Coast, and immersed myself in the California lifestyle. I spend most of my free time outdoors hiking, exploring, lounging at the beach, cooking, and getting involved in the Central Coast wine industry. Though I am still in the process of fulfilling my dreams, every day I get a little closer. As they say in the south, "Laissez les bons temps rouler (Let the good times roll)!"

Maggie Thompson
Lake Michigan's freshwater runs in my veins, covered with corn-husk skin. I spent the first eighteen years of my life in the Mitten State, and there I learned the Midwest way of life: *Work hard, be kind.* My family has always been very supportive of me. I wouldn't be able to be away from them if it wasn't for our constant communication. I moved to attend Cal Poly in San Luis Obispo after I was accepted into the Wine and Viticulture program. My efforts to leave a chemical city in the middle of Michigan in order to go to school on the West Coast have allowed me to spend ample time outside farming, hiking, and playing on the beach. I dream of moving back to Michigan after I finish my education to work at a microbrewery on a Great Lake coast. For now, though, I'm enjoying the sunshine, the people, and all the adventures that come my way.

Tal Edelstein
This piece describes my transition as an Israeli in Israel, to a proud Israeli in America. I still consider Israel my home, in large part due to the huge number of family members I have there. At the age of twelve, I moved with my family to northern Los Angeles county in California, where I spent most of my time playing basketball and focusing on academics. I was admitted to Cal Poly San Luis Obispo and am now finishing my freshman year of college as a Business Administration major.

Tara Baumann
Writing is therapy. Breakthroughs and breakdowns are inevitable in each; except typically in writing, nobody is on the other side of the room to pass you a tissue and write you a prescription for more Klonopin. I like writing poetry, singing, and acting. I was studying animal science at Cal Poly in San Luis Obispo when I wrote this paper, but I'm now pursuing musical theater studies at Cal State Fullerton. Music and writing make me feel most centered. I also enjoy cooking and I love animals. I have a poodle named Poodle, and he's been with me on the best and worst of days.

Made in the USA
San Bernardino, CA
21 November 2016